THE DICKENS PANTOMIME

F. Bernard, "My First Pantomime—When Grandfather Took Us Children to Sadler's Wells," from the *Illustrated London News*, December 23, 1876.

THE DICKENS PANTOMIME

EDWIN M. EIGNER

University of California Press
Berkeley · Los Angeles · London

University of California Press
Berkeley and Los Angeles, California

University of California Press, Ltd.
London, England

© 1989 by
The Regents of the University of California

Library of Congress Cataloging-in-Publication Data

Eigner, Edwin M.
    The Dickens pantomime / Edwin M. Eigner.
      p.   cm.
    Includes index.
    ISBN 0-520-06255-8 (alk. paper)
      1. Dickens, Charles, 1812–1870—Knowledge—Performing arts. 2. Dickens, Charles, 1812–1870—Criticism and interpretation. 3. Pantomime (Christmas entertainment) in literature. 4. Pantomime (Christmas entertainment)—History. 5. Performing arts—Great Britain—History—19th century. 6. Comic, The, in literature. I. Title.
PR4592.P45E34   1989   88-17391
823'.8—dc 19

Printed in the United States of America
1 2 3 4 5 6 7 8 9

Contents

Acknowledgments vii
Preface ix

1. The Comic Business 1
2. Mixed Sweets 21
3. The Benevolent Agent and Her Pious Fraud 46
4. Pantaloon: Some Dickensian Parents 69
5. Dandy Lover: Death and the Gentleman 91
6. Harlequin: The Guilty Hero 105
7. Columbine: A Pure Woman 130
8. Clown: The Triumph of the Dickensian Absurd 143

Conclusion: The Death of the Clown 169
Index 179

Acknowledgments

I owe a debt of gratitude to several people who shared with me their extensive knowledge of nineteenth- and twentieth-century pantomime. Michael Booth of the University of Victoria has been patient in explaining some of the differences between pantomime and melodrama, as has David Mayer III of the University of Manchester, who generously lent me a part of his considerable library of pantomime scripts. John Morley, the most prolific of modern pantomime writers, and Denis Martin, who has for many years produced and directed nineteenth-century pantos at the Players' Theatre in London, were both gracious and wonderfully informative. A number of American Victorianists, including Fred Kaplan, U. C. Knoepflmacher, Peggy Stamon, and Garrett Stewart, encouraged me by responding enthusiastically to my excitement with the subject of Dickens and pantomime, thus helping to validate it for me. Ruth Eigner, my panto-going companion both by marriage and inclination, also helped in this regard. Such encouragement is invaluable and beyond thanks.

I have tried to acknowledge with citations throughout the text some part of what I owe to previous and current critics of Dickens. Indeed it may be felt that I have quoted too frequently from the great library of Dickens interpreters, but my conception of the activity in which I engage is that it consists of a conversation among readers, and I have therefore attempted to get as many relevant voices as possible into the discussion. Certainly I have learned by listening to all of them.

The Guggenheim Foundation and the University of California were generous with financial support.

I am grateful for the collections of printed pantomimes and

of unpublished pantomime manuscripts at the British Library and the Huntington Library and for the collection of pantomime programs at the Library of The British Theatre Association. I am also indebted to the helpful librarians and for the materials at the Theatre Collection at Harvard, the Humanities Research Library at the University of Texas, and the libraries of the University of California at Los Angeles, San Diego, and Riverside. Nancy Eigner, Ruth Eigner, Carla McGill, Barbara Ras, Teresa Saul, Sharon Tyler, and Kathleen Van Deusen assisted with editing, checking, and proofreading.

My greatest debt is to Murray Baumgarten and John Jordan, who let *me* assist *them* in founding the Dickens Project of the University of California. Under their direction the Dickens Universe has become a model for a vitally nurturing intellectual community. The encouragement and good advice I received over the years from them and from the students and the international faculty at the yearly winter conferences at Riverside, Santa Barbara, San Diego, and the University of Texas at Austin and at the longer summer meetings at Santa Cruz first fostered my thoughts on the Dickens pantomime and later helped me see them through to a conclusion. It is to Murray and John, therefore, and to the Dickens Universe that this work is dedicated.

Preface

After more than two hundred and fifty years pantomime remains an essential and vital part of the British Christmas season and a financial staple of most English and Scottish theaters. Indeed it is questionable if there would be much theater, at least outside of London, if there were no pantomime in December and January to pay the debts of the old year and start off the new one comfortably in the black. Foreigners like myself usually need to be told that this sort of entertainment has nothing in common with the delicate subtleties of French mime—that it is in fact raucous, graceless, and excessively talkative. Foreign parents should perhaps be advised that while panto is definitely children's theater, it trades on mildly dirty jokes and sexually suggestive routines. Most classicists already know that the form is in no way related to the Roman *pantomimus,* a single actor impersonating all the characters of a story, for the English panto is performed by a full cast of actors and actresses of various sorts, only some of whom will know even their own parts; and there will be nothing at all classical about the entertainment. English audiences have apparently needed to be told each year for at least the last two hundred that the pantos of today are not nearly as good as those of the past but that they are still very much worth going to.

Citations to *David Copperfield* are to the Clarendon Edition of 1981, edited by Nina Burgis. Citations to Dickens' other novels are to the Clarendon editions currently in print, i.e., *Pickwick Papers, Oliver Twist, Martin Chuzzlewit, Dombey and Son, Little Dorrit,* and *The Mystery of Edwin Drood.* Where no Clarendon edition exists as yet, citations are to the New Illustrated Oxford Edition. All citations to Dickens' novels are made parenthetically in the text, and except in the case of *David Copperfield,* where only page references are given, they include reference to both pages and chapters.

Pantomime is illegitimate theater, despised and disdainfully avoided by many serious theatergoers and frequently resented, from the time of David Garrick, by some artistic theater managers compelled by financial considerations to accommodate such productions. It continues, nevertheless, to influence the imagination of British and Irish children, and before radio and television, when it usually provided a child's first experience of dramatic presentation, the influence was often formative. Nor in the nineteenth, as in the twentieth century, did the children, at least some of them, stop going to the panto when they grew up, although the more self-conscious adults may have felt it necessary to bring a child along. Thackeray never outgrew his love for pantomime, and its influence on his writing, as on that of Joyce, is unmistakable. Charles Dickens, who is the focus of this study, remained both a delighted spectator and a serious critic of pantomime throughout his life, and, as I shall try to show, its characters, its situations, and its structures were etched deeply into the essentially dramatic and theatrical nature of his creative imagination, so deeply that the dramatis personae of his novels, the movement of his plots, and even the meaning of his vision can all be understood in terms of pantomime conventions.

Most of the discussions that follow will have to do primarily with the characters, themes, and situations in *David Copperfield*, but since my purpose is to provide a new reading of the entire canon, or at least a new approach to Dickens, I shall deal with all the novels either in passing or in detail. The pantomimic imagination is central to each of them, and, indeed, I began considering the Dickens pantomime in articles on *Great Expectations* and *A Tale of Two Cities*. I focus here on *David Copperfield* not so much because it was and remained the author's favorite work but because that novel provides a number of subplots, each illustrating an interesting variation of the basic pantomime structure and of the constellation of pantomime characters—Harlequin, Columbine, Pantaloon, Dandy Lover, Clown, and the benevolent Agent—which usually inhabit and inform a Dickens novel. *David Copperfield* is a representative work in that it comes at the middle of the author's writing career and is the eighth of his fifteen novels. It also separates his early fiction from what has been called the dark Dickens and thus provides an opportunity for speculation regarding this crucial change of vision.

But the major reason for my concentration on *David Copperfield* is the presence there of Wilkins Micawber, who is at once Dickens' greatest comic creation and his most significant adaptation of the Clown, the figure that Joseph Grimaldi had developed into the ruling, the most energetic and energizing, character in the Christmas pantomime. Any study of Dickens' comedic vision, it seems to me, must confront Micawber. Indeed, the failure to do so has been a sadly acknowledged deficiency in much Dickens criticism during the last generation. J. Hillis Miller was reduced to treating Micawber in a digression, and many others of the American school of psychological and symbolic Dickens criticism feel apologetic about the inability of their approach to deal with Dickens' great comic characters.[1] One English critic, A.O.J. Cockshut, prefaces his discussion of *David Copperfield* with an apology relating specifically to Micawber:

> Everybody can appreciate Mr. Micawber, but what can the critic say about him? All criticism naturally tends to concentrate on the topics about which the most interesting things can be said. No doubt these topics tend to coincide, in a rough and ready way, with the greatest literary achievements. But there are exceptions. To read Mr. Micawber is, as Chesterton said, like receiving a blow in the face. It is a deeply felt experience, but it is not susceptible of analytical description. It follows that any detailed critical discussion of *David Copperfield* will tend to be unbalanced because it is impossible to give appropriate space to Micawber.[2]

Perhaps even Dickens failed to give Mr. Micawber appropriate space. Indeed, I have sometimes found myself wishing

---

1. J. Hillis Miller, *Charles Dickens: The World of His Novels* (Cambridge, Mass.: Harvard University Press, 1958), pp. 150–51.
2. A.O.J. Cockshut, *The Imagination of Charles Dickens* (New York: New York University Press, 1962), p. 114.

that Queen Victoria had ordered Boz to write a story about Micawber in love. This study, however, provides an approach that may help restore the critical balance by placing Micawber at the center of the Dickensian vision and by then relating him to all the hilarious, sad, or tragic clowns both in *David Copperfield* and throughout the other novels.

1

The Comic Business

We are all actors in The Pantomime of Life.
—Charles Dickens

"How different were the Christmas pantomimes of my younger days!" lamented James Robinson Planché, whose brilliantly successful extravaganzas of the second and third quarters of the nineteenth century did more perhaps than anything else to change the character and form of the English pantomime. "All the tricks and changes had a *meaning*, and . . . there was as regular a plot as might be found in a melodrama."[1] Well, perhaps not quite. Pantomime has thrived on absurdity from its beginnings in the early eighteenth century to the present day, when it remains an enormously popular British entertainment.[2] Innovation has always been so powerful an imperative to the producers of this form of drama that despite the talk every Christmas season about "trad"

---

1. James Robinson Planché, *Recollections and Reflections* (London: Samson Low, Marston, 1901), pp. 339–40.
2. In *Oh, Yes It Is: A History of Pantomime* (London: British Broadcasting Corporation, 1985), Gerald Frow estimates that in the 1984–85 Christmas season there were more than thirty pantos produced in and around London, seventy in the provinces, and twenty-two in Scotland. Some ran from mid-December to March. "For many theatres," Frow writes, "the pantomime is the one copper-bottomed, financially successful certainty of the entire production calendar" (p. 181). John Morley, the most prolific and highly respected of modern pantomime writers, says that hundreds of his plays are produced by British groups scattered throughout the world, and I have seen a creditable production of his *Robinson Crusoe*, performed by an American company for an American audience in Riverside, California. Morley is quoted in the *Observer Magazine* of 24 December 1978 as calling Pantomime "our National Theatre. The French have the Comédie-Française; we have the Pantomime" (interview by Alan Road, p. 27).

elements, regularity of any sort is difficult to find. Nevertheless the Victorians—not only Planché, but most nineteenth-century commentators—looked back to the Regency pantomime of Joseph Grimaldi as the period when the wild confusion had something like a rational form. "This is the simple story," wrote Andrew Halliday in 1867, "of Clown, Pantaloon, Harlequin, and Columbine."[3] "A pretty story," Planché called it:

> A nursery tale, dramatically told, in which "the course of true love never did run smooth," formed the opening; the characters being a cross-grained old father, with a pretty daughter who had two suitors—one a poor young fellow, whom she preferred, the other a wealthy fop, whose pretentions were of course favoured by the father. There was also a body servant of some sort in the old man's establishment. At the moment when the young lady was about to be forcibly married to the fop she despised, or on the point of eloping with the youth of her choice, the good Fairy made her appearance and, changing the refractory pair into *Harlequin* and *Columbine*, the old curmudgeon into *Pantaloon*, and the body servant into *Clown*, the two latter, in company with the rejected Lover, as he was called, commenced the pursuit of the happy pair, and the "comic business" consisted of a dozen or more cleverly constructed scenes, in which all the tricks and changes . . . were introduced as contrivances to favour the escape of *Harlequin* and *Columbine*, when too closely followed by their enemies. There was . . . an interest in the chase [which] increased the admiration of the ingenuity and the enjoyment of the fun of the tricks by which the runaways escaped capture, till the inevitable "dark scene" came—a cavern or a forest in which they were overtaken, seized, and the Magic Wand which had so uniformly aided them snatched from the grasp of the despairing *Harlequin*, and flourished in triumph by the *Clown*. Again, at the critical moment the protecting Fairy appeared, and, extracting the consent of the father to the marriage of the devoted couple, transported the whole party to what was really a grand last scene. . . . There was some congruity, some dramatic construction in such pantomime.[4]

---

3. Andrew Halliday, "About Pantomimes," in *Mixed Sweets from Routledge's Annual* (London: George Routledge, 1867), p. 47.
4. Planché, *Recollections and Reflections*, pp. 136–38.

What Planché refers to as "the comic business" was sometimes called the "harlequinade." This zany, largely wordless, part of the pantomime survived throughout the nineteenth century but was progressively truncated and disconnected from the plot structure. Before being abandoned altogether in our own century, it was kept on only as an obligatory and boringly tasteless afterpiece, sponsored by the tradesmen whose shops were advertised in the stage settings. The harlequinade became totally unnecessary to the plot because the problems of the young people had already been solved within the "opening," which had expanded during the course of the century from a few short introductory scenes into much more than a full-length play. By the 1890s, certainly, and probably by the 1870s, the harlequinade had been demoted into a variety of satyr play, performed so late in the evening that most of the audience had gone home or else to sleep. Indeed, as early as 1846 a writer for *The Illustrated London News* complained of the harlequinade that "not one person in one hundred has the slightest idea what Harlequin and Columbine, Clown and Pantaloon, are running about after. All their connection with the opening legend is entirely lost sight of, and so little is cared what becomes of them or where they go, because there are no motives shown for their various shifts."[5] But in Planché's youth, as in Charles Dickens', the comic business—its absurdity connected to the love story in a way that seemed somehow to make sense, at least in retrospect—was the very soul of pantomime.[6]

Dickens' fascination with pantomime was as great, perhaps, as his general interest in the theater and equally long-

---

5. Quoted in Frow, *Oh, Yes It Is*, p. 103.
6. As late as 1863, the pantomime writer in Andrew Halliday's sketch, "My Pantomime," published in the 14 November issue of Dickens' *All the Year Round*, is told, "You see, the people at this house don't listen much to the opening: they're always impatient for the comic business. . . . The people here, you see, usually whistle through the opening. When they get tired of whistling, they shy ginger-beer bottles and pull up the seats" (p. 274). A couple decades later, they were pulling on their coats when the harlequinade began.

lasting. Even today, as I have said, most British and Irish children experience their first live theater at the pantomime. Dickens dated his own enthusiasm for the stage from "the period when I believed the Clown was a being born into the world with infinite pockets";[7] and when Dickens came to rewrite the memoirs of Joseph Grimaldi, the greatest of pantomime clowns, he recalled the traveling pantomimes of Richardson's wagons as providing his own first theatrical experience, and he remembered shortly afterwards being brought up to London "from remote country parts in the dark ages of 1819 and 1820 [when he was seven and eight] to behold the splendour of the Christmas Pantomimes and the humour of Joe."[8] Dickens was informed that on this occasion he clapped his "hands with great precocity," and the rest of his life bears witness that the child's delight in the pantomime never did fade.

In his maturity, Dickens frequently attended what he called the "pankelmime,"[9] and he associated, sometimes on terms of friendship, with many people connected with these popular entertainments. He knew most of the writers—Planché, Nelson Lee, J. B. Buckstone, Robert Brough, E. L. Blanchard—indeed, some of them, like Mark Lemon and Gilbert à Beckett, were members of his circle and actors in his own amateur theatricals. His dear friend Clarkson Stanfield had been one of the great pantomime scenic designers. George Augustus Sala, another friend, became perhaps the most noted of pantomime reviewers. Dickens' sympathy with even the less respectable members of this world is evident from a letter of 1860 describing one of several encounters with down-and-out pantomime actors:

> The other day, there . . . appeared before me (simultaneously with a scent of rum in the air) one aged and greasy man, with a

---

7. Speech to the General Theatrical Fund Association, 6 April 1846, in *The Speeches of Charles Dickens*, ed. K. J. Fielding (Oxford: Oxford University Press, 1968), p. 76.

8. Quoted in John Forster, *The Life of Charles Dickens*, ed. J.W.T. Ley (London: Cecil Palmer, 1928), p. 104.

9. Letter to Mark Lemon, 25 December 1849, *The Letters of Charles Dickens*, ed. Graham Storey and K. J. Fielding (Oxford: Clarendon Press, 1981), 5:680.

pair of pumps under his arm. He said he thought if he could get down to somewhere (I think it was Newcastle), he would get "taken on" as a Pantaloon, the existing Pantaloon being "a stick, sir—a mere muff." I observed that I was sorry times were so bad with him. "Mr. Dickens, you know our profession, Sir—no one knows it better, Sir—there is no right feeling in it. I was Harlequin on your own circuit, Sir, for five-and-thirty years, and was displaced by a boy, Sir—a boy!" [10]

Besides rewriting the *Memoirs of Joseph Grimaldi* for publication, Dickens contributed articles on the pantomime to each of the general magazines he edited from the 1830s through the 1860s, *Bentley's Miscellany, Household Words,* and *All the Year Round,*[11] and he encouraged the writing of similar articles by Andrew Halliday and others.[12] The word *pantomime,* used both as a noun and as a verb, occurs throughout his writings. David Copperfield goes to the pantomime; so does Pip, Dickens' other autobiographical self-portrait; and Nicholas Nickleby is introduced to the members of the Vincent Crummles theatrical company by the pantomime actor Mr. Folair. From *Pickwick Papers* to *The Mystery of Edwin Drood,* pantomimists perform and pantomimes are acted.[13]

In recent years virtually all of Dickens' works have been interpreted in relation to pantomime by such critics as J. Hillis Miller, who has written that "allusions to pantomimic gestures . . . are fundamental in the text of the *Sketches [by Boz],*"[14] and Michael Hollington, who suggests the usefulness of a study of the many references to pantomime in *A Tale of*

10. Letter to Mary Boyle, 28 December 1860, quoted in *The Dickens Theatrical Reader,* ed. Edgar Johnson and Eleanor Johnson (London: Victor Gollancz, 1964), p. 337.

11. These articles are "The Pantomime of Life," *Bentley's Miscellany* 1 (1837): 291–97; "A Curious Dance Round a Curious Tree," *Household Words* (17 January 1852): 385–87; and "A Sermon in the Britannia Theatre," *All the Year Round* 2 (1860): 416–21.

12. Ella Ann Oppenlander lists ten articles on pantomime and pantomime characters in her *Dickens's* All the Year Round: *Descriptive Index and Contributor List* (Troy, New York: Whitston, 1984).

13. See Paul Schlicke, *Dickens and Popular Entertainment* (London: Allen and Unwin, 1985), pp. 138–39.

14. J. Hillis Miller, "The Fiction of Realism: *Sketches by Boz, Oliver Twist,* and Cruikshank's Illustrations," in *Charles Dickens and George Cruikshank: Papers Read at a Clark Library Seminar on May 9, 1970, by J. Hillis Miller and*

Two Cities "and their possible relation to the novel's structure, which seems to parallel or parody the two halves of a traditional pantomime."[15] Most recently (1987) H. Philip Bolton has noted in an introduction to *Dickens Dramatized*, his bibliography of dramatic adaptations of Dickens' works, that some of the material he has discovered "strongly suggests that Dickens' books may be fruitfully interpreted in the light of the archetypes of the contemporary British harlequinade or pantomime."[16] But the influence of the pantomime on Dickens has been obvious to critics from as early as 1834, when the reviewer for *The Sun* compared the "broad, rich farce" of the sketch "The Steam Excursion" to the "spirit of Grimaldi."[17] And in 1871 Margaret Oliphant noted that "the atmosphere of 'Pickwick' is more like that of a pantomime than any other region we know." Oliphant went on to say, "Never was there such a big, full, crowded pantomime stage—never so many lively changes of scene and character."[18] A generation later, George Bernard Shaw made a similar observation, also with reference to *Pickwick Papers*, interpreting virtually the entire novel as an extended harlequinade:

David Borowitz (Los Angeles: William Andrews Clark Memorial Library, 1971), p. 67.

15. Michael Hollington, *Dickens and the Grotesque* (Sydney: Croom Helm, 1984), p. 121. Other useful works on Dickens and pantomime include William Axton, *Circle of Fire: Dickens' Vision and Style and the Popular Victorian Theatre* (Lexington: University of Kentucky Press, 1966); Joseph Butwin, "The Paradox of the Clown in Dickens," *Dickens Studies Annual* 5 (1976): 115–32; Helen Lorraine Kensick, "The Influence of the Pantomime Clown on the Early Novels of Charles Dickens" (Ph.D. diss., University of Massachusetts, 1984); Charles Wolfe, "Dickens and the Theatrum Mundi" (Ph.D. diss., University of Kansas, 1967); and A. L. Zanbrano, *Dickens and Film* (New York: Gordon Press, 1977). A paper by Coral Lansbury, "Pecksniff and Pratfalls," delivered first at the New York meeting of the Modern Language Association, 29 December 1984, and later at the Dickens Theatre Conference at Austin, Texas, 31 January 1986, deals with the pantomime Clown in Dickens.

16. H. Philip Bolton, *Dickens Dramatized* (Boston: G. K. Hall), p. 61.

17. See Kathryn Chittick, "Pickwick Papers and the Sun, 1833–1836," *Nineteenth-Century Fiction* 39 (1984): 331.

18. Margaret Oliphant, " Charles Dickens," *Blackwood's Edinburgh Magazine* 109 (1871): 679, 681.

Jingle, Job, Sam Weller and the Fat Boy form a harlequinade pure and simple, in which Mr. Pickwick himself, in spite of the affection which Dickens conceived for him as he warmed to his work, and as success encouraged him to take himself seriously, figures as the king of pantaloons. Our love and esteem for the "angel in tights and gaiters" must not blind us to the fact that Mr. Pickwick repeatedly gets drunk, and is tumbled head over heels, knocked about with fire-shovels and carpet bags, cuffed, cheated, mulcted, duped, haled before the magistrate, put in the pound, and pelted with turnips and rotten eggs, not to mention mistaking a lady's bed for his own and getting into serious trouble in consequence. But it must be confessed that the Pickwickian harlequinade, as a harlequinade, is incomparable.[19]

My own previous work on the subject has been along lines similar to those suggested by Shaw.[20] It has been concerned with how the various characters of the harlequinade—Harlequin, Pantaloon, Lover, Clown, and Good Fairy—appear as in a configuration around Columbine not only in *Pickwick Papers* but also in many of the novels that follow. I argue for a more systematic scheme than Shaw, I feel sure, would allow. Thus, if I were writing about *Pickwick Papers,* I would try to follow the pantomime story as we have seen it summarized by James Robinson Planché. If we think of Miss Rachel as a burlesque Columbine, then Mr. Tupman becomes the foppish Lover, and Jingle plays the agile but penniless trickster, Harlequin. Once Columbine and Harlequin run off together, both Pickwick and Mr. Wardle fall into place as Pantaloons and are soon joined in their awkward pursuit by the body servant, Clown, Sam Weller. After a quick, comic chase this situation resolves itself with the typical harlequinade capture and escape, in which Harlequin as usual proves himself far too nimble for his self-righteous but heavy-footed pursuers. The superfluous Pantaloon and his ward return now to Dingly

---

19. George Bernard Shaw, *Daily Chronicle* (London), 14 April 1892. Reprinted in *Shaw on Dickens,* ed. Dan H. Laurence and Martin Quinn (New York: Frederick Ungar, 1985), pp. 23–24.
20. See *Dickens Studies Annual,* 11, 12, and 14.

Dell, but the "comic business" does not end at this stage. Rather, Jingle pursues new Columbines through a variety of rapid scenes, while Pickwick and his amusing Clown blunder after them. The rejected Lover has been dropped from the cast, but his is anyway, as we shall see, an optional part in the harlequinade; and a second Clown, Harlequin's servant, a role in the pantomime invented for Grimaldi's son, appears as Job Trotter. The "dark scene," where Pantaloon and his Clown momentarily triumph over Harlequin, takes place, of course, in the Fleet prison and is followed by a transportation to what Planché called "a grand last scene." All that is missing is the Good Fairy or Benevolent agent, a role that Pickwick himself plays in the concluding action and for which, in all subsequent Dickens novels, he was to provide the chief model.

Shaw regarded the Pickwick pantomime as "mere schoolboy Tomfoolery," a wonderful but "thoughtless heehaw" which Dickens outgrew when he "realised that the people who so tickled his sense of the ridiculous were human beings like himself, and that the merry Eatanswill game was being played not for fun, but for solid plunder, the cost of which in human life and happiness no man could calculate."[21] I take the Dickens pantomime much more seriously, seeing in it the essential pattern of Dickens' comedy, the basis for his psychological insights and his social vision, as well as the modus operandi of his aesthetics.

For one thing, the slapstick of the harlequinade provided the absurdity that, as Northrop Frye has shown, was Dickens' great contribution to the pattern of classical New Comedy. Frye describes this pattern as follows:

> The main action is a collision of two societies which we may call for convenience the obstructing and the congenial society. The congenial society is usually centered on the love of hero and heroine, the obstructing society on the characters, often parental, who try to thwart this love. For most of the action the thwarting characters are in the ascendant, but toward the end

---

21. *Shaw on Dickens*, pp. 24–25.

a twist in the plot reverses the situation and the congenial society dominates the happy ending.[22]

Frye suggests that Dickens derived this formula from the comedies of Ben Jonson, but although Jonson is an undeniable influence, the pantomime opening offers an even more immediate one, while the pantomime harlequinade provides the creative absurdity, which is not to be found in Jonson and which gives Dickens' vision, according to Frye, its special anarchical quality.[23]

This anarchy is the essence of the harlequinade. "In nineteenth-century farce," writes Michael Booth, "man is initially responsible for his own absurd predicament, although chance and an implacable universe drive him inexorably thereafter over the edge of comic catastrophe." But in the Regency harlequinade:

> Man's plight is often created by the transformation, misbehaviour, and relentless hostility of objects and mechanical devices: things are not what they seem to be, or rather they are, but then they change frighteningly into something else. Nothing can be relied on; the very ground itself dissolves under the feet of the helpless characters. Such comedy is almost cosmic in its implications; audiences were really laughing at the yawning gulfs in man's own life. As is usual in extreme forms of comic theatre, a terrible seriousness underlies the jollity and "animal spirit" of pantomime that Leigh Hunt so much admired.[24]

Booth's is a brilliant description of the precarious sense of imbalance that the harlequinade used to effect, but we need not, I think, adopt so grim a view of it. Nor was Frye encouraging us to see the anarchical absurdity in Dickens

---

22. Northrop Frye, "Dickens and the Comedy of Humors," in *Experience in the Novel: Selected Papers from the English Institute,* ed. Roy Harvey Pearce (New York and London: Columbia University Press, 1968), p. 52.
23. Frye, "Dickens and the Comedy of Humors," p. 80.
24. Michael Booth, "Introduction to Volume Five," in *English Plays of the Nineteenth Century,* vol. 5, *Pantomimes, Extravaganzas and Burlesques,* ed. Michael Booth (Oxford: Oxford University Press, 1976), pp. 7–8.

as an expression of cosmic despair. On the contrary, he felt it was time for literary criticism to rescue the concept of the absurd from disillusioned theologians,[25] as in fact literary criticism, belatedly registering the influence of Mikhail Bakhtin, was on the verge of doing, and, more recently still, of relating both to Dickens[26] and to the pantomime. Thus, Louisa E. Jones, writing from a Bakhtinian perspective, notes the "carnival violence, linked to patterns of ritual sacrifice and rebirth . . . in 19th-century [French] pantomime. However extreme, it expands boundaries, ignores limits, overrides taboos, even that of death. It is always, in the end, revitalizing, an exuberance in which everyone participates and which everyone survives."[27] Long before or independently of the influence of Bakhtin, the historian of English pantomime, A. E. Wilson, had written to glorify the chaos of this Christmas and Easter entertainment as "a release of pure animal spirits," an expression of "the spirit of carnival and of the Saturnalia."[28] And Richard Findlater, the twentieth-century biographer of Grimaldi, had described the harlequinade Clown as "a Cockney incarnation of the saturnalian spirit; a beloved criminal, free from guilt, shame, compunction, or reverence for age, class or property."[29]

Such views of pantomime influenced by, or at least compatible with, Bakhtin's theories of the carnivalesque seem more reasonable in light of my own experience with the genre as reader and spectator than reactions based on theories of the romantic grotesque, and they seem better to describe

---

25. Frye, "Dickens and the Comedy of Humors," p. 80.
26. Hollington, *Dickens and the Grotesque*.
27. Louisa E. Jones, *Sad Clowns and Pale Pierrots: Literature and the Popular Comic Arts in 19th-Century France* (Lexington, Ky.: French Forum, 1984), p. 21.
28. A. E. Wilson, *Pantomime Pageant: A Procession of Harlequins, Clowns, Comedians, Principal Boys, Pantomime-writers, Producers and Playgoers* (London: Stanley Paul, n.d.), p. 14.
29. Richard Findlater, *Joe Grimaldi: His Life and Theatre* (Cambridge: Cambridge University Press, 1978), p. 160. Another commentator, Robert F. Storey, writes, "In the pantomimes the Regency has left us, Clown reigns in a bizarre and fabulous world, the stability of which is never certain" (*Pierrot: A Critical History of a Mask* [Princeton: Princeton University Press, 1978], p. 90).

what Dickens was able to derive from pantomime and its tradition. William Axton, whose *Circle of Fire: Dickens' Vision and Style and the Popular Victorian Theatre* remains in some ways the best work on its subject, would agree:

> "Dark" grotesque, which Mark Spilka among others has found to be an important strain in Dickens' vision, was largely absent from the nineteenth-century popular theater, aside from an occasional pantomime "dark scene." Rather, the drama best known to Dickens—and, as we shall see, Dickens' own work—located its interest principally in that aspect of grotesque comedy to which we have given the name of burlesquerie . . . a comedy of discontinuity and incongruity which had no clear and final satiric intention, although it made use of all the usual comic and satiric devices. Broad humor, mixed fantasy and realism, bustling and inconsequential action, ludicrous caricature, extraordinary costume, setting and property—these are the materials of nineteenth-century burlesque.[30]

Moreover, Axton sees burlesque and other nineteenth-century comedic forms that grew out of pantomime as performing a social function similar to the functions of the Bakhtinian carnivalesque and of Frye's creatively absurd, though he refers to neither concept specifically. According to Axton, these forms of theater aim "to do away with familiar footholds . . . [and] to unsettle perspectives derived from tradition and convention."[31] Classical New Comedy in its pure form tends to confirm these perspectives by allowing the young lovers to establish themselves at last as the legitimate heirs of the societal institutions used against them earlier. When they have children of their own and have learned the ways of the world they have inherited, the new middle-aged pair will be as bad as their parents ever were. But the pantomime harlequinade and the creatively absurd of Dickens anarchically create spaces that permit the characters on the stage, as well as the audience watching them, to imagine fresh and original patterns of human relationships. Harlequin and Columbine do

---

30. Axton, *Circle of Fire*, pp. 30–31.
31. Ibid., p. 32.

not inherit the old world; they create a new one or they recreate a paradise that far antedated the society of their parents.

This liberating function may explain why modern pantomime, with the old harlequinade elements absorbed into its nursery tale plot, remains such an essential part of the Christmas season in Britain and why Dickens' *A Christmas Carol* has become an obligatory element of Christmas in America: In these two Protestant cultures they are all we have left of carnival, that regenerative and essential medieval tradition that allowed the spontaneity and freedom necessary for the rethinking of traditions. According to Bakhtin, the carnival-grotesque operated to consecrate such inventive holidays from hierarchical thought

> to permit the combination of a variety of different elements and their rapprochement, to liberate from the prevailing point of view of the world, from conventions and established truths, from clichés, from all that is humdrum and universally accepted. This carnival spirit offers the chance to have a new outlook on the world, to realize the relative nature of all that exists, and to enter a completely new order of things.[32]

In his book *Dickens and Popular Entertainment*, Paul Schlicke sees Dickens' achievement as motivated by his desire to preserve elements of popular culture that had allowed for spontaneity but had come under serious official attack from early in his career. Schlicke has little to say about pantomime, and he does not refer to Bakhtin, but he points out that there never was a time when the carnival spirit was in greater danger than at the beginning of the Victorian period. "Most modern historians are convinced," he notes, "that the nadir of English popular culture was reached during the 1830s, the very time Dickens began writing about it."[33]

As the new editor of *Bentley's Miscellany* in 1837, Dickens printed a piece by William Jerdan on Richardson the Showman and Bartholomew Fair, the great carnivalesque extrava-

---

32. M. M. Bakhtin, *Rabelais and His World*, trans. Helene Iswolsky (Bloomington: Indiana University Press, 1984), p. 34.
33. Schlicke, *Dickens and Popular Entertainment*, p. 5.

gance at Smithfield, which, having survived such formidable Puritan enemies as represented by Ben Jonson's Zeal-of-the-Land Busy, was shortly to be abolished by the Victorians after more than seven hundred vital and vitalizing years. The tone of Jerdan's article is elegiac, both regarding the great impresario of pantomimes and other popular entertainments and the penny theater world he represented:

> At length, alas! his days—his fair days—were numbered, and, as the song says, "the good old man must die." As his first, so his last exhibition at Smithfield; but Smithfield, like the other national theatres [the vanishing urban fairs of England] shorn of its splendour, degenerate, and degraded. It seemed . . . the last of the fairs—others had been abolished and put down— and this, the topmost of them all, was sinking under the march of intellect, the diffusion of knowledge, and the confusion of reform. Fairs in Britain were ended, and it was not worth Richardson's while to live any longer.[34]

Not so, of course, the young Dickens. Thus, a month later, in March 1837, when he exuberantly published his own first piece on the pantomime, and under his own familiar pen name, there was nothing even vaguely elegiac about Boz's "The Pantomime of Life."

> Before we plunge headlong into this paper, let us at once confess to a fondness for pantomimes—to a gentle sympathy with clowns and pantaloons—to an unqualified admiration of harlequins and columbines—to a chaste delight in every action of their brief existence, varied and many-coloured as those actions are, and inconsistent though they occasionally be with those rigid and formal rules of propriety which regulate the proceedings of meaner and less comprehensive minds. We revel in pantomimes.

He insists, moreover, that the value of pantomime consists not in its madcap irrelevance to life but in its capacity to provide a *theatrum mundi*:

> A pantomime is to us, a mirror of life; nay more, we maintain that it is so to audiences generally, although they are not aware

34. William Jerdan in *Bentley's Miscellany* 1 (February 1837): 184.

of it; and that this very circumstance is the secret cause of their amusement and delight.[35]

Before the essay concludes, he is ready to make the same confident claims for pantomime that Shakespeare had made for the stage in general. I shall be arguing later that no one since Shakespeare believed so strongly as Dickens did in the power of his art over the hearts and minds of the audience. Here Dickens presents himself modestly in relationship to his great precursor as one "tracking out his footsteps at the scarcely-worth-mentioning little distance of a few millions of leagues behind." Nevertheless, he quotes the famous line of Jacques from *As You Like It* and presumes "to add, by way of a new reading," that Shakespeare "meant a Pantomime, and that we are all actors in The Pantomime of Life."[36]

The association Dickens insists on between pantomime and our everyday lives is essential in terms of the carnivalesque in his work. Bakhtin makes the point that "carnival is not a spectacle seen by the people; they live in it . . . while carnival lasts . . . subject only to . . . the laws of its own freedom." Clowns and fools "were the constant accredited representatives of the carnival spirit in everyday life out of carnival season . . . not actors playing their part on a stage."[37]

In his introduction to the *Memoirs of Joseph Grimaldi*, written in the year following "The Pantomime of Life," Dickens recalls his own childish though "intense anxiety" to know what clowns "did with themselves out of pantomime time, and off the stage."

> As a child, we were accustomed to pester our relations and friends with questions out of number concerning these gentry;—whether their appetite for sausages and such like wares was always the same, and if so, at whose expense they were maintained; whether they were ever taken up for pilfering other people's goods, or were forgiven by everybody because it was only done in fun; how it was they got such beautiful complexions, and where they lived; and whether they were

35. Boz, "The Pantomime of Life," *Bentley's Miscellany* 1 (March 1837): 291.
36. Ibid., 297.
37. Bakhtin, *Rabelais*, pp. 7–8.

born Clowns, or gradually turned into Clowns as they grew up. On these and a thousand other points our curiosity was insatiable. Nor were our speculations confined to Clowns alone: they extended to Harlequins, Pantaloons, and Columbines, all of whom we believed to be real and veritable personages, existing in the same forms and characters all the year round.[38]

On the other hand, Dickens valued pantomime precisely because of its differences from everyday life, of which the most meaningful for him was the magic of a world where seemingly realistic violence had no real or lasting consequences. Thus he wrote in 1849 that like the sadism in the Punch and Judy show, pantomime was "quite harmless in its influence." Moreover, "One secret source of the pleasure very generally derived from . . . the more boisterous parts of a Christmas Pantomime, is the satisfaction the spectator feels in the circumstance that likenesses of men and women can be knocked about without pain or suffering."[39] After witnessing three more pantomime seasons, Dickens developed this same thought in an article for *Household Words*. There he celebrated "that jocund world of Pantomime," where there is no affliction or calamity that leaves the least impression:

> Where a man may tumble into the broken ice, or dive into the kitchen fire, and only be the droller for the accident; where babies may be knocked about and sat upon, or choked with gravy spoons, in the process of feeding, and yet no Coroner be wanted, nor anybody made uncomfortable; where workmen may fall from the top of a house to the bottom, or even from the bottom of a house to the top, and sustain no injury to the brain, need no hospital, leave no young children; where every one, in short, is so superior to all the accidents of life, though encountering them at every turn, that I suspect this to be the secret (though many persons may not present it to themselves) of the general enjoyment which an audience of vulnerable spectators, liable to pain and sorrow, find in this class of entertainment.[40]

38. Charles Dickens, introduction to *Memoirs of Joseph Grimaldi* (London: Richard Bentley, 1838), 1: xi–xii.
39. Letter to M. E. Taylor, 6 November 1849, *The Letters of Charles Dickens*, 5: 640.
40. Dickens, "A Curious Dance Round a Curious Tree," pp. 385–86.

By the time he reached the last decade of his career and of his life, Dickens would claim, in "A Sermon in the Britannia Theatre," that the pantomime was an essentially moral form. Moreover, an unidentified writer for Dickens' journal of the 1860s, *All the Year Round*, attempted to reconcile the typical harlequinade mixture of realism and fantasy by concluding that "pantomime is truth—truth coloured, condensed, elaborated—but truth itself."[41] But in the 1830s and the 1840s when life was filled for him with interesting ambiguities, Dickens was able to live comfortably with the nourishing confusions of pantomime.[42]

I shall discuss some of these confusions in subsequent chapters. Ambiguities persist, for instance, in Dickens' attitudes toward the various pantomime characters, especially when he associated them with his own persona, as in the case of Harlequin, or when he based them on his always problematic father, as with Pantaloon and Clown. After John Dickens' grisly death, moreover, Charles Dickens' attitudes changed dramatically, so that a Dick Swiveller or a Wilkins Micawber is no longer a possible character for him, and a pathetic Lord Frederick Verisopht hardens, as Branwen Pratt has pointed out, into a tragic Sydney Carton.[43]

Nevertheless, beginning as early as *Nicholas Nickleby* (1838), the cast of characters in the Dickens pantomime remains relatively stable. There is always at least one heroine in the situation of the ingenue of the pantomime opening. With the willful contrivance or ignorant cooperation of a parent or parent figure, she is drawn toward marriage with or exposed to

---

41. "Paradise Revisited," *All the Year Round* 15 (1866): 31.

42. It is one of the curiosities of literary history, but perhaps a significant one, that Keats seems first to have thought of the concept of negative capability as he was walking home from a pantomime performance. Since Keats did not like the pantomime he had seen, he might dislike my crediting it for his idea, but Bakhtin might say that such breakthroughs are to be expected after even poor carnival experiences.

43. Branwen Bailey Pratt traces the line beginning with Lord Frederick through Carton to Eugene Wrayburn in "Carlyle and Dickens: Heroes and Hero-Worshippers," *Dickens Studies Annual*, ed. Michael Timko, Fred Kaplan, and Edward Guiliano, 12 (1983): 243.

seduction by an unsuitable lover. And, of course, she is truly in love with a poor but decent lad, like Colin in the pantomime, who is later transformed into Harlequin. But while this young man may look like a hero and would seem to be Columbine's probable rescuer from the clutches of his villainous rival, he always fails, both in Dickens and in the pantomime, and the rescue must come from a Benevolent Agent or, more frequently, from the least likely of all the characters in the dramatis personae, the Clown, the part in the Regency pantomime that Grimaldi had raised to the position of preeminence.

As opposed to the purer harlequinade configurations we observed in *Pickwick Papers,* the constellation of pantomime characters surrounding Madeline Bray of *Nicholas Nickleby* illustrates the pattern that was to persist in Dickens' novels from the late 1830s. Columbine is no longer a spinster whose romantic ambitions, inappropriate to her time of life, render her a figure of fun. Instead she is a loving daughter prepared to suffer the fate worse than death for the sake of a selfish Pantaloon, who has none of the lovable virtues of a Pickwick or a Wardle. Instead of the foolishly romantic Mr. Tupman, Columbine is menaced now by lecherous Arthur Gride, the hoary old miser, who salivates at the prospect of enjoying his dainty morsel of a bride. Nicholas, Columbine's rightful protector, anguishes about her situation, but, like Harlequin in the post–Grimaldian pantomime, he has lost much of his magic and most of his agility. In fact, if it were not for the clownish Newman Noggs, and if Dickens had not taken care to provide twin Benevolent Agents, the Cheeryble brothers, the story might have ended sadly indeed.

Another pattern is illustrated in the constellation of male characters surrounding Kate Nickleby, who is also a threatened Columbine. Ralph Nickleby plays the guilty Pantaloon in relation to his niece, and the melodramatic villain, Sir Mulberry Hawk, is the unsuitable lover to whose unwanted attentions Ralph exposes her. Frank Cheeryble takes the part of the attractive, well-meaning but largely ineffective Harlequin. There is nothing the matter with his courage, or indeed with the courage of any of Dickens' Harlequins: Frank bravely defends the honor of a lady whom he does not know and who never appears in the novel. But he does nothing for Kate except to marry her in the end. Meanwhile, the rescue of Kate's honor comes from, of all places, the foolish dissipate, Lord Frederick Verisopht, who gives up his life, effectively clearing her good name.

After *Nicholas Nickleby* the pantomime cast remains constant, at least in the early novels, and with little change in the basic characteristics of the figures. How wedded Dickens had become to the pattern is clear in *The Old Curiosity Shop*, where the changes in the plot, dictated by the need to expand the original short story into a novel, also mandated a shift in the pantomime roles. Thus Paul Schlicke writes of Kit Nubbles:

> Kit . . . is introduced in the opening scene in the immediately recognizable role of clown. Master Humphrey describes him as "a shock-headed shambling awkward lad with an uncommonly wide mouth, very red cheeks, a turned-up nose, and certainly the most comical expression of face I ever saw." And he concludes his description by reporting that Kit was "the comedy of the child's life." Dickens evidently changed his mind almost at once about the boy's function in the story, for Kit soon sheds his near-idiocy and becomes Nell's faithful but largely ineffectual champion. In later chapters he is noteworthy not for Grimaldi-like antics but for cheerful and earnest devotion to duty.[44]

In other words, and according to the terms we have been using, Clown has become Harlequin. In fact nearly all the characters change their pantomime roles. In the original configuration, where Kit Nubbles was Clown, Nell's elder brother was the oppressive parent-figure, who sought for mercenary reasons to force an unsuitable marriage to Dick Swiveller, the Dandy Lover of these early passages. After the plot revision,

---

44. Schlicke, *Dickens and Popular Entertainment*, p. 101.

however, Old Trent takes his grandson's place as a different kind of faulty parent; Quilp becomes the unsuitable lover, based, perhaps, on the most terrible of pantomime lovers, the Yellow Dwarf,[45] which was a Grimaldi vehicle of 1821; and Swiveller, as Paul Schlicke also notes, moves into the space of Clown, just vacated by Kit Nubbles. In this more grateful role the ne'er-do-well tippler becomes a man of action, a worthy successor in the line of Clowns already begun by Newman Noggs and Lord Frederick Verisopht and to be fully realized comically in the person of Wilkins Micawber and, as previously noted, tragically in that of Sydney Carton.

In his essay, "The Argument of Comedy," Northrop Frye explains how Shakespeare rejected the New Comedy conventions of Plautus and Terence in favor of a profounder pattern of comedy, "the ritual of death and the revival that also underlies Aristophanes, of which an exact equivalent lay ready to hand in the drama of the green world," as practiced by his Elizabethan predecessors and contemporaries.[46] In another essay, "Dickens and the Comedy of Humors," previously referred to, Frye concluded that this tradition was not available to the more urban Dickens, who had therefore to seek out *his* profounder pattern in the creatively absurd.

Dick Swiveller, in his second identity as pantomime Clown, and all the related characters who rescue the heroines of the succeeding novels and stories illustrate where Dickens chose to look for his nonsense and just how much this choice freed him to achieve. The pantomime was perhaps not so strange a place to seek the vanished green world of the Elizabethans, as at least two significant commentators have noted. Martin

---

45. Toby Olshin in " 'The Yellow Dwarf' and *The Old Curiosity Shop*," *Nineteenth-Century Fiction* 25 (1970): 96–99, makes a good case for the Mother Bunch fairy tale as a source for the character, but he does not mention the frequent appearance of the lecherous dwarf in nineteenth-century pantomime.

46. Northrop Frye, "The Argument of Comedy," in *Shakespeare: Modern Essays in Criticism*, ed. Leonard Dean (New York: Oxford University Press, 1957), p. 85. Abstracted from *English Institute Essays 1948, 1949* (Columbia University Press).

Meisel has written that the grand transformation scene in pantomime "was a manifestation of the prelapsarian world, full of beauty and wonder, benign influences, overgrown vegetation, and visionary palaces."[47] G. K. Chesterton long ago instructed us that "if what we want is Merry England, our antiquarians ought not to revive the Maypole or the Morris Dancers; they ought to revive Astley's and Sadler's Wells and the old solemn Circus and the old stupid Pantomime, and all the sawdust and all the oranges."[48]

And this is precisely what, throughout his career, Charles Dickens chose to do. The revival of popular entertainment, as we have heard Paul Schlicke say, was a major concern with him. In the succeeding chapters I hope to show why this was the case and how one particular form of popular entertainment, the Christmas pantomime, with its redeeming figure of the Clown, was central to the artistic as well as to the moral vision of Dickens.

---

47. Martin Meisel, *Realizations: Narrative, Pictorial, and Theatrical Arts in Nineteenth Century England* (Princeton: Princeton University Press, 1983), p. 184.

48. G. K. Chesterton, *Appreciations and Criticisms of the Works of Charles Dickens* (London: J. M. Dent & Sons, 1911), pp. 61–62.

2

Mixed Sweets

> The best actors in the world, either for tragedy, comedy, history, pastoral, pastoral-comical, historical-pastoral, tragical-historical, tragical-comical-historical-pastoral, scene individable, or poem unlimited. Seneca cannot be too heavy nor Plautus too light. For the law of writ and liberty, these are the only men.

Bakhtin writes that "every genre has its methods and means of seeing and understanding reality," and that "the artist must learn to see reality with the eyes of the genre."[1] I should like to modify this statement slightly and suggest that frequently it is the genre in which the artist has chosen to write, whether for practical reasons or because of prevailing literary fashions or for some other cause, that teaches him his reality. Thus the genre in which the artist writes, whatever it is, will more or less dictate the world he or she will be able to perceive. To state the obvious, no writer can produce a tragedy, in the true sense of the word, without expressing a tragic worldview, because the form acts as a lens, focusing, so to speak, the artist's view of the world. The same could be said of comedy, satire, elegy, and various subgenres of lyric poetry. The question of mixed genres, like tragicomedy, however, has vexed modern criticism and literary theory. Do the two views meld into a unified romance vision, or do they provide a nonauthoritarian double vision, which is confusing and/or liberating? Do they undermine one another, or does

---

1. M. M. Bakhtin and P. N. Medvedev, *The Formal Method of Literary Scholarship*, trans. A. J. Wehrle (Baltimore: Johns Hopkins University Press, 1978), pp. 133–34.

the one worldview replace and contradict its rival? And what about pantomime, which was born in the eighteenth century as a form alternating scenes of the pretentiously serious and the absolutely zany, and which continued and indeed continues to display an inexhaustible capacity for incorporating multitudes of formal contradictions and for reincorporating any and all of the many dramatic subgenres it has generated over the years—the extravaganza, the review, the burlesque, and the melodrama, to name only a few?

The pantomime that Planché saw as containing "some congruity, some dramatic construction,"[2] was the two-part pantomime, most probably invented by Sheridan in 1781 for *Robinson Crusoe; or, Harlequin Friday*.[3] Horace Walpole, who was accustomed to watching the older form in which, as I have said, bits of harlequinade alternated on a regular basis but without plot connection with scenes of stuffy, neoclassical mythology, was shocked at the disunities in this innovation:

> How unlike the pantomimes of Rich, which were full of wit, and coherent, and carried on a story. . . . How Aristotle and Bossu, had they ever written on pantomimes, would swear! It was a heap of contradictions and violations of the costume. *Friday* is turned into Harlequin, and falls down at an old man's feet that I took for Pantaloon, but they told me it was *Friday's* father. I said "Then it must be *Thursday*," yet it still seemed to be Pantaloon. I see I understand nothing from astronomy to a harlequin-farce![4]

This confusion is understandable, for what Walpole saw were characters changing not only their identities but also their generic allegiance at the touch of a wand. The basic form of the new pantomime soon became standard and lasted for over a

---

2. See chap. 1, p. 2.
3. Frow, *Oh, Yes It Is*, p. 57.
4. Letter to the Countess of Upper Ossory, 3 November 1782, *Letters of Horace Walpole*, ed. Mrs. Paget Toynbee (Oxford: Clarendon Press, 1903), 12: 359. John Rich, referred to in the quotation, was the manager of Covent Garden in the early eighteenth century. He was the first significant pantomime producer in England and the first great Harlequin.

hundred years, but even after theatergoers got used to the transformations and the abrupt shift from one kind of play to another (sometimes with the substitution of an entirely new company of actors), there remained and developed sufficient discontinuities and contradictions to maintain the audience in a state of chaotic uncertainty.

The pantomime of his youth that Planché described seemed to be a relatively straightforward business of a play dissolving from a realistic beginning into a fantastic conclusion. The "opening" of a Regency pantomime can be called realistic, however, only in comparison with "the comic business" that follows. The first scenes were, after all, usually based on a fairy tale, and most of the characters wore masks or grotesque papier-mâché faces called "big heads" and spoke in a highly artificial rhymed verse. This part of the pantomime can be termed realistic only because usually nothing of the overtly supernatural occurs in it; because the laws of gravity seem still to be in effect; and because the commercial values of what the audience would call "the real world" appear to rule: That is to say, romantic love is being crushed by mercenary interest. None of these realities hold once the harlequinade commences, and we begin now to question whether they ever were realities. From this point Harlequin's wand can reasonably transform sofas into pigsties; chairs can fly up into the air, separating an astounded Clown from the dinner he had been ready to consume; and the agile lover can always make a fool of the wise old head who pursues him. But just as curiously, the mise-en-scène has as suddenly become incongruously contemporary: Margate, London Bridge, Stamford Hill, the Bank of England, New Cross, with a View of the Railroad, the Albert Gate, the Woolwich Dockyards,[5] and so on. As Michael Booth writes, "Pantomimes . . . were very aware of the railroad age and the industrial scene. Factories, ware-

---

5. The first five settings occur in Charles Farley, *Harlequin and Mother Bunch; or, The Yellow Dwarf* (Covent Garden, 1821); the others are from John M. Morton, *Guy, Earl of Warwick; or, Harlequin and the Dun Cow* (Covent Garden, 1841). In contrast, the opening is set at Warwick Castle in medieval times.

houses, docks and railway stations appear in pantomime scenes."[6] It is like an early silent film by Chaplin, where the slapstick, certainly derived from the harlequinade, is played on the drab streets of a city that is not only modern but also appears to have proceeded from the imagination of a naturalist like Zola.

Chaplin's source could as easily have been Dickens. Martin Meisel has written that the visual jokes of the harlequinade, characteristic of this "most surreal and spectacular of nineteenth-century theatrical forms, link the powerful graphic tradition that passed into nineteenth-century visual art in its 'low' forms (Gillray, Heath, Cruikshank) with the curious imagination of Dickens and the madness of the early cinema."[7] William Axton has argued that Dickens was influenced by disparities between scenic background and action in pantomime from as early as *Sketches by Boz*, where "the settings are of real places . . . uniformly described in a carefully documented, realistic manner, even though the action that takes place in front of this backdrop is as wildly fantastic as any caper of Harlequin or Pantaloon."[8] Indeed the entire world of *Sketches* is pantomimic in its confusions. Michael Hollington has written that it is "dynamic, electric, and alive in its startling juxtapositions and incongruous transitions."[9]

Moreover, although pantomime is presumed to be an escapist form of drama, both parts have always bristled with topical allusions. In the 1820s, for example, Grimaldi satirized fops in the character of Dandy Lover.[10] *The Times* wrote during this same period that "the effect of a pantomime very much depends on the introduction of the reigning follies and extravagant inventions of the day."[11] More than one hundred sixty years later a 1985–86 theatrical press release announced

---

6. Booth, "Introduction," *English Plays of the Nineteenth Century*, 5: 49.
7. Meisel, *Realizations*, p. 123.
8. Axton, *Circle of Fire*, p. 47.
9. Hollington, *Dickens and the Grotesque*, p. 43.
10. See David Mayer III, "Dandyism in Regency Pantomime," *Theatre Notebook* 19 (1965): 90–100.
11. Quoted in Frow, *Oh, Yes It Is*, p. 136.

that *Micromania* "retains the most popular features of a traditional pantomime. . . . but [its] Jack and Jill are computer fanatics, like all self-respecting eleven year olds, and with a chorus of people called Input and Output, Control, Byte and Bugs Boggins they outwit the baddies. 'Matrix, monitor and mainframe,' chants the Demon King."[12]

"Allusions to current events," wrote Henry Morley in 1853, "are the life of a pantomime."[13] It would be difficult, however, to say just what is not its life. Like a baggy and voracious Dickens monster of a novel, it not only makes room for everything but also makes everything into itself by a species of artistic digestion. The classical unities, satirized by Dickens as early as *Nicholas Nickleby*[14] and ignored throughout his career, are made a mockery of in the sprawling, digressive, multiscened pantomime of the nineteenth century.

As Axton has written, the pantomime Dickens knew was "a curious amalgam of fantasy, realism, topicality, anachronism, grotesquerie, burlesque, spectacle, music, verse, dance, and a serious story. Moreover, it bequeathed most of its mixed elements to the dramatic forms that grew out of it."[15] One can go further, as I am certain Axton would agree, and say that pantomime reinherited many of these mixed elements after they had been modified by their new owners. The relationship between pantomime and melodrama, the two most popular forms of nineteenth-century theater, is interesting in this regard. The two genres aimed at somewhat different audiences and worked on different emotions, and, most

---

12. Jane Dewey, *Micromania* (The Questors Theatre).
13. Henry Morley, *The Journal of a London Playgoer* (Leicester: Leicester University Press, 1974), p. 66.
14. In chapter 24, Mr. Curdle, the literary critic, insists on "the unities of the drama, before everything," but when pressed to define them, he "coughed and considered. 'The unities, sir,' he said, 'are a completeness—a kind of universal dovetailedness with regard to place and time—a sort of general oneness, if I may be allowed to use so strong an expression. I take these to be the dramatic unities so far as I have been enabled to bestow attention upon them, and I have read much upon the subject, and thought much. . . . I don't know whether I make myself understood'?" (pp. 311–12).
15. Axton, *Circle of Fire*, p. 20.

significantly for our purposes, facilitated entirely different worldviews. Nevertheless it is generally agreed that melodrama in France developed out of the pantomime.[16] In England, where there remains some debate over the genealogy, it is at least safe to say that some of the best-known writers in the one genre—Buckstone and the Dibdens, for instance—frequently achieved equal fame in the other. As a result, pantomime and melodrama felt free to borrow situations from one another and to lend characters back and forth.

The Bad Baron of the modern panto is an obvious example of a pantomime character—Lover or Dandy Lover—who attained his full stature in the melodrama but who would have been left stranded if the more enduring pantomime had not still been around to welcome him back when melodrama died. The presence of this character in both pantomime and melodrama makes it difficult to say whether Dickens' villains like Sir Mulberry Hawk of *Nicholas Nickleby*, James Carker of *Dombey and Son*, and Tulkinghorn of *Bleak House* are derived from one form or the other or from both. As we shall see later on, the answers to such questions make for important differences of critical interpretation.

There are also similarities between the hero of melodrama and Harlequin and between the heroine and Columbine. An even greater confusion exists regarding the Comic Man of melodrama and the pantomime Clown. Which, for instance, is Newman Noggs of *Nicholas Nickleby*? He doesn't eat enough for a pantomime Clown, although he does drink; but he isn't brave enough for a Comic Man, either. Like the Comic Man, he is the hero's friend, but like the Clown, he works for the villain. The business of Noggs' hiding in the closet and overhearing the plot against Madeline Bray is taken straight out of the melodrama, as Dickens acknowledged years later when he put just such an incident into the parody melodrama in *Great Expectations*. However, Newman's penchant for pan-

---

16. See Frank Rahill, *The World of Melodrama* (University Park and London: Pennsylvania State University Press, 1967), pp. 22–38.

tomimic gestures, particularly the imaginary punches directed at Ralph Nickleby, belong to Clown, as do the particulars of his appearance:

> He was a tall man of middle-age with two goggle eyes whereof one was a fixture, a rubicund nose, a cadaverous face, and a suit of clothes (if the term be allowable when they suited him not at all) much the worse for wear, very much too small, and placed upon such a short allowance of buttons that it was marvellous how he contrived to keep them on. . . . Noggs . . . rubbed his hands slowly over each other: cracking the joints of his fingers, and squeezing them into all possible distortions. The incessant performance of this routine on every occasion, and the communication of a fixed and rigid look to his unaffected eye, so as to make it uniform with the other, and to render it impossible for anybody to determine where or at what he was looking, were two among the numerous peculiarities of Mr. Noggs. (Chap. 2, pp. 8–9)[17]

Nicholas's other friend, John Browdie, the big Yorkshireman, acts, looks, and talks more like a Comic Man, but there is enough of this beloved figure from the melodrama in Noggs to make us conclude either that the two genres were conflated in Dickens' mind or that he wanted both genres to be present in the minds of his readers.

I believe that the second of these conclusions can be argued at least for the novels after *Nicholas Nickleby*, but I am impressed with the way that Dickens, even in that early, exuberant, and unplanned novel, appears from the structure to

---

17. Kensick, who has written a dissertation on "The Influence of the Pantomime Clown on the Early Novels of Charles Dickens," remarks on Noggs' "frantic pantomimic performances":

> Noggs can barely contain his irrepressibly animated body. . . . Noggs systematically prefers the wilder forms of silent expressivity to any form of language. Like his prototype the pantomime clown, he introduces an element of nonsensical behavior which is designed to disrupt the everyday world. . . . Noggs cannot function very well or for any sustained period of time in the context of the everyday world. He is never really part of it, i.e., no one is able to interact with him in a way that makes any sense. As a foil against the cunning and greed of Ralph, he has a large role to play and he stays in character as a clown virtually all the time. (Pp. 49, 104–5)

be using genres self-consciously. Thus in roughly the first quarter of *Nicholas Nickleby* Dickens appears to be writing a kind of social melodrama or exposé, similar to the form he was currently producing over the way in *Oliver Twist*. Then after Squeers has been beaten the novel settles into the mode of satire in the Kenwigs chapters and into that of parody in the Vincent Crummles section, especially parody of romantic melodrama, in which the Crummleses specialize. But this foolishness turns deadly serious in the third quarter of the novel, when Sir Mulberry menaces Kate, and Ralph Nickleby, the arch-villain, joins in the plot against Smike.

Finally, in the last four monthly numbers of the novel the most significant generic transformation in the Dickens pantomime occurs. Although there is still plenty of melodrama left, after the introduction of the Cheerybles the novel becomes in essence a love story; pathos and sentiment, not anger, are now the ruling emotions. Smike dies, not a victim of oppression and social neglect, but a hopeless lover. The Madeline Bray plot, although its rhetoric is the most melodramatic in the novel, is a perfect pantomime opening. Ralph Nickleby does not leave the stage muttering curses as he had done in an earlier section; he hangs himself out of remorse and grief for the lost son. Lord Frederick Verisopht, as we have seen, begins a line of sentimental action that will culminate twenty years later in Sydney Carton's act of sacrificial love. And the novel itself concludes with no fewer than three marriages. A significant alteration that the French melodrama made when it developed from the pantomime, writes Louisa E. Jones, was to replace "the final festive marriage with the punishing of a villain."[18] In the melodramatic second and third quarters of his novels Dickens seems to be preparing us for just such a structure. But in the fourth quarter, the old pantomime, with its comic ending, always reasserts itself.

George J. Worth, writing about melodrama, shows that *Dombey and Son* contains two sets of characters and that the

---

18. Jones, *Sad Clowns and Pale Pierrots*, p. 49.

members of the one group demonstrate their moral superiority to the others by their unsuitability to melodramatic treatment. Thus "Dickens' use of melodramatic devices . . . helps to drive home this all-important contrast between the two groups of characters."[19] Axton has shown how Dickens changes even his basic narrative rhythms in this same novel when shifting from one genre to the other. In the railroad passages, "The elaborate manipulation of almost every rhythmic resource of syntax, rhetoric, and repeated motif operates upon the episode with the same emotional force as their musical counterparts in an old-fashioned melodrama." In the chapter containing Carker's death there is "a complexly orchestrated climacteric of prose rhythms that, like a well wrought piece of symphonic music, brings together a host of lesser themes and variations with which prose style has been playing a deliberate game of development since the introduction of the railroad motif and its associated measures early in the novel." When Dickens shifts from melodrama to sentiment, however, the style is governed by entirely different prose rhythms.

> The pace is slower, syntax is somewhat simpler, although parallelism and periodicity continue; and repeated refrains in image and motif often are the means of effecting a pathetic indirection. In *Dombey and Son,* the determining rhythms for such scenes are not derived from the terrific beat of rushing trains but rather from the more languid measures of ocean waves, in token of the fact that the protagonists of these episodes are allied with those eternal values associated with the sea, as opposed to the time-bound materialists such as Dombey and Carker who are linked to the rhythms of the railroad.[20]

Indeed, by the time of *Dombey and Son* the general pattern observed in *Nicholas Nickleby* of changing genres every five

---

19. George J. Worth, *Dickensian Melodrama* (Lawrence: University of Kansas Humanistic Studies, 1978), pp. 94–96.
20. Axton, *Circle of Fire,* pp. 251–52.

installments has become precise. Paul Dombey, to whom the first or pathetic quarter has belonged, dies at the end of the fifth number. At this point in the succeeding twenty-part novels David Copperfield's youthful ordeal ends as his aunt decides to adopt him; Jo shows Lady Dedlock to the burial ground in Tom-all-Alone's; Arthur Clennam resigns Pet Meagles to Henry Gowan while John Chivery, the sad clown of *Little Dorrit,* writes his own epitaph; and while John Harmon of *Our Mutual Friend* stumps "overhead in the dark, like a Ghost," muttering bitterly of Bella Wilfer, "So insolent, so trivial, so capricious, so mercenary, so careless, so hard to touch, so hard to turn" (bk. 1, chap. 16, p. 208), the Boffins are finding it sticky going in "The Dismal Swamp." During the next two quarters, the middle of the novels, the melodrama grows, at first somewhat comically, and then, following the catastrophe of the "keystone," the precise center of a Dickens novel, it takes on greater and greater seriousness until the fifteenth number, when a melodramatic climax is reached. In *Dombey and Son* the second quarter has to do with Dombey's curious courtship, grotesquely managed by Cleopatra and Major Bagstock, the comic Mephistopheles, whereas the third quarter becomes grim as Carker pursues his relentless seduction of Edith. The eleventh number of *Dombey and Son* begins the quarter of the novel in which the melodramatic vision finds its most serious expression. This third section starts with a chapter emblematically entitled "The Wooden Midshipman Goes All to Pieces." It ends in the fifteenth number with a melodramatic chapter called "The Thunderbolt," where Edith's elopement with Carker appears to have fully realized the novel's potential for chaos.

During the second quarter of the next novel David Copperfield has his first dissipation and falls into puppy love with a succession of unsuitable women, culminating in his comically presented falling in love at first sight with Dora. Then following the elopement of Emily and Steerforth at the center of the novel, all the women seem to fail or, like Agnes pursued by Heep, are placed in the gravest danger. David is disappointed in Dora, and the troubles in Annie Strong's marriage, hinted at in the fifth number, climax in the fifteenth, as Annie vindicates her honor in a grandly staged melodramatic scene.

This third quarter is always the place where the moral universe of a Dickens novel shakes on its foundations. In *Bleak House*, for instance, Jo dies, Richard becomes the victim of Mr. Vholes, and Tulkinghorn closes in on Lady Dedlock and is murdered. Bucket, the real detective, takes over in the final chapter of the fifteenth number, whereas in the second quarter of the book we had been amused by the antics of the parody detectives, Mr. Guppy and Mrs. Snagsby. In *Little Dorrit* during the third quarter the family degenerates in Italy as redemptive power seems to drain out of Amy, and at home Mr. Merdle's complaint becomes the condition of England. At the very conclusion of the section "Mr. Dorrit and his matchless castle were disembarked among the dirty white houses and dirtier felons of Civita Vecchia, and they scrambled on to Rome as they could, through the filth that festered on the way" (chap. 18, p. 616). Finally, in *Our Mutual Friend* Boffin's supposed degeneration, which began just after the center of the novel, appears to be complete, and Eugene Wrayburn, having stooped to the bribing of Mr. Dolls, helplessly sets out to destroy himself and the woman he loves. Bradley Headstone is in angry, vengeful, melodramatic pursuit.

In the shorter novels of this period—*Hard Times, A Tale of Two Cities*, and *Great Expectations*—where a three-part structure governs, it is once again the middle section that contains the significant doubt. To Mrs. Sparsit and to the reader Louisa Bounderby appears to be descending a moral staircase. After a lifetime of evasions and repressed guilt feelings Charles Darnay, born Evrémonde, is drawn to the "Loadstone Rock" of his destruction (bk. 2, chap. 24, p. 223). In the final chapter of the "Second Stage of Pip's Expectations" Magwitch unexpectedly materializes out of the stormy night of the hero's troubled conscience. In all three novels the time has arrived, it would appear, for melodramatic revenge, vengeance against the heartless social philosophers of *Hard Times*, the exploitive social order of *A Tale of Two Cities*, and the guilty self of *Great Expectations*.

What seems billed to be the penultimate moment of melodrama, however, turns out instead to be the Dark Scene of pantomime, for in the final sections of both the three- and the four-part novels, doubt is resolved not so much through action, although this is where the great climaxes occur, but through sentiment. Florence Dombey flees the thunderbolt and the breast-crushing hand of her father to find her way to the loving safety of Captain Cuttle and the Wooden Midshipman. Although there is melodramatic satisfaction for the reader in the gory death of Carker, what truly liberates is the comic self-sacrifice of Mr. Toots, the novel's pantomime Clown. In *David Copperfield* the death of Steerforth might have provided a pathetic catharsis, if Dickens had not chosen instead to use it, along with the death of Dora, as an occasion for a course of grief that David must endure. Moreover, Micawber's rebellion, as we shall see later on, is a climax that at least equals the power of these catastrophes and that serves more emphatically than they to rescue the novel from the power of death, represented by Uriah Heep, the grave-digger's son. *Little Dorrit* ends with a series of stunning jailbreaks from all the social, economic, religious, and psychological prisons of the earlier sections. In *Hard Times* Dickens relies at last on the unsophisticated faith of Stephen Blackpool and the embarrassingly impractical emotions of the circus people. *A Tale of Two Cities* concludes with the comic loyalty of Miss Pross and the sentimental sacrifice of Sydney Carton. *Our Mutual Friend* ends with a romantic Eugene Wrayburn and a comically benevolent Nicodemus Boffin. Everywhere in the late novels (except in *Great Expectations,* one of the few works for which Dickens was unable to imagine a happy ending), impending melodrama gives way, like a scenic transformation effected by some Benevolent Spirit's magic wand, to sentimental comedy, the province of pantomime. Both are genres derived from the theater, but they generate remarkably different worldviews.

It used to be generally felt that Dickens' penchant for melodrama was a serious liability to his art, and some otherwise favorable readers still squirm during the sentimental scenes and the highly rhetorical speeches. Earle Davis wrote that "if Dickens deserves a place in the ranks of great novelists," then the Chestertonian view of him as a great melodramatist "must be rejected fiercely. Melodrama is always artistically inferior to authentic tragedy."[21] And Worth, whose valuable book promises to make a case for *Dickensian Melodrama*, usually concludes that the less melodrama in a novel the better that novel is. More recently Grahame Smith has taken a different view. "Dickens," he writes, "is probably the last great literary artist in the English tradition for whom melodrama is a completely serious business. . . . His brilliant intelligence perceives it as an aspect of his social and personal world . . . and his artistry embodies it in forms that give it the status of imaginative truth as well as social insight."[22]

This new, favorable treatment of the melodramatic aspects of Dickens' art is consistent with some recent studies that take melodrama itself more seriously. Robert B. Heilman, for instance, has insisted that the vision of melodrama is to be found not only "in a silly and meretricious form, [as] in a cinema or television thriller," but also "with dignity and power" in such works as *The Trojan Women, Romeo and Juliet, The Nigger of the Narcissus, War and Peace, Richard III,* and *The Duchess of Malfi.* What distinguishes both these masterpieces of the ages and nineteenth-century theatrical melodramas from tragedy itself is essentially that in them "man is pitted against a force outside of himself—a specific enemy, a hostile group, a social force, a natural event, an accident or coincidence." Heilman states that "melodrama is the principal vehicle of protest and dissent; or, more accurately, it is the vehicle of protestants and dissenters when they are in a polemic rather than a soul-searching mood," and that, when put to this use, the emotion it exploits is indignation.[23] Peter Brooks includes Balzac, Henry James, Dickens, Gogol, and Dos-

---

21. Earle Davis, *The Flint and the Flame: The Artistry of Charles Dickens* (London: Victor Gollancz, 1963), p. 62.
22. Grahame Smith, *The Novel and Society: Defoe to George Eliot* (London: Batfort Academic and Educational, 1984), p. 189.
23. Robert B. Heilman, *Tragedy and Melodrama: Versions of Experience* (Seattle and London: University of Washington Press, 1968), pp. 79, 96–97.

toevsky among "the social melodramatists" of nineteenth-century fiction, noting that it is far from an accident that melodrama should have been born in Paris during the French Revolution.[24]

As it was inherited by Dickens, the worldview of melodrama is one of anger, articulated, Christopher Prendergast has pointed out, "largely through the systematic use of two elementary rhetorical figures, antithesis and hyperbole."[25] As this view gradually comes into focus during the middle sections of a Dickens novel, at first comically and then with greater and greater seriousness, the reader fills with rage at characters like Ralph Nickleby and Mr. Dombey, who are ironically the unwitting victims of a commercial system they seek to exploit. In later novels like *Bleak House* and *Little Dorrit*, the reader's rage is aimed more directly at the evil system itself and only secondarily at its representative among the dramatis personae. Smith writes that Dickens' "discovery . . . of the fictional institution—Chancery, the Circumlocution Office, the Marshalsea—as the focus of social insights in a purely artistic form is one of the greatest advances made by the nineteenth-century novel," and he relates it to the "discovery—no other word is appropriate—. . . that the forms of existence characteristic of his period (the complex interdependencies of Victorian capitalism and the street life of the great metropolis are two of the most obvious) lend themselves to melodramatic treatment because they carry the seeds of melodrama within them."[26]

In the anger-filled, inflated, black and white worldview of melodrama, these seeds always seem to promise a bitter harvest. From as early as *Oliver Twist* Dickens was a master at encouraging such an expectation, at working up the blood with a skill that has been the envy of any number of Marxist

---

24. Peter Brooks, *The Melodramatic Imagination: Balzac, Henry James, Melodrama, and the Mode of Excess* (New Haven and London: Yale University Press, 1976), pp. 22, 43–44.
25. Christopher Prendergast, *Balzac: Fiction and Melodrama* (London: Edward Arnold, 1978), p. 7.
26. Smith, *The Novel and Society*, pp. 182, 189–90.

and feminist writers and other melodramatists with political agendas. He is also famous, or notorious, for disappointing these expectations. Arnold Kettle has argued that plot overcomes pattern in *Oliver Twist* so that the social system, which was at first correctly recognized as the child's enemy, ends up protecting him from Fagin, another of society's victims.[27] Dombey is forgiven in the final number, while his rebellious wife is left in social exile. And it has been widely noted how in *Barnaby Rudge* and *A Tale of Two Cities* Dickens turns away in fear and disgust from the revolutions that the logic of these novels had established as just or inevitable or both. But indeed, as the title of the second book of *Hard Times* indicates, whatever "Reaping" of the bitter harvest there is to be takes place not at the climax but considerably before it. The third and final book of *Hard Times* is called "Garnering," and, as we have seen, it is governed by much softer sentiments than anger.

Such turnabouts have been seen by some critics as symptomatic of Dickens' psychological confusions and by others as indicative of his essential allegiance to bourgeois values. In both interpretations a failure of nerve is suspected. No one wants to argue anymore that these changes of direction took place while Dickens was in the act of writing, for the pattern repeats itself throughout his career and there is too much evidence to show that he planned most of his books carefully in advance. Thus if he turns away from the excesses of the French Revolution in "Book the Third" of *A Tale of Two Cities*, they did not take him by surprise, and he knew from the beginning that he would ultimately have the reader mounting the scaffold of sentimental self-sacrifice with Sydney Carton rather than the barricades of revengeful self-assertion with Madame Defarge. Nevertheless many readers remain convinced that the one man of the nineteenth century best able to perceive and express the need for political reform habitually

---

27. Arnold Kettle, "Dickens: *Oliver Twist*" in *An Introduction to the English Novel*, Volume 1 (London and New York: Hutchinson's University Library, 1951), 1: 123–38.

stopped short of inciting it, that he did not recognize, or did not choose to exploit, what Heilman calls the "public function" of melodrama: to concentrate "energies for the rigors of combat, whether for war or its moral equivalents."[28]

Heilman writes that "novelists of two centuries and four countries have noted the way in which indignation may be used toward [such] an end."[29] And surely Dickens, the most skillful and effective of social melodramatists, understood the power of his craft and genre to effect political change. What he may have doubted was the significance of the change melodramatic anger might inspire. In his essay on "Charles Dickens," George Orwell writes that because "there is always a new tyrant waiting to take over from the old," two views are tenable in regard to revolution: "The one, how can you improve human nature until you have changed the system? The other, what is the use of changing the system before you have improved human nature? They appeal to different individuals . . . the moralist and the revolutionary, [who] are constantly undermining one another."[30] Orwell sees Dickens as a moralist, albeit an angry one, but a moralist without any plan for changing the hearts and minds of his readers. I disagree with the last part of this conclusion, but I suppose it is typical of our realistic century that we underrate the power of sentiment as much as we overrate the effect of melodrama.

Later on in the same essay Orwell observes that "most revolutionaries are potential Tories, because they imagine that everything can be put right by altering the *shape* of society; once that change is effected, as it sometimes is, they see no need for any other."[31] Melodrama is conservative in a somewhat different way. It appears to threaten the moral order of things, but it serves ultimately to confirm it. As Prendergast explains:

---

28. Heilman, *Tragedy and Melodrama*, p. 129.
29. Ibid., p. 130.
30. George Orwell, "Charles Dickens," in *Dickens, Dali and Others* (New York and London: Harcourt Brace Jovanovich, 1973), p. 23.
31. Ibid., p. 71.

> All the formal apparatus of melodrama—the unfolding of mysteries, providential confidences, hyperbolic gestures, stereotyped characters, antithetical patternings—participates in the articulation of this stable and reassuring universe. The dominant function of melodrama appears, therefore, to be that of making available an uncomplicated moral reading of the universe, and of locating the subject in a secure world of moral representations, free from doubt, uncertainty and ambiguity.[32]

Prendergast's book is primarily about Balzac, but he illustrates his point about the essentially conservative nature of melodrama with reference to the murder of Nancy in *Oliver Twist*, one of the few works of Dickens that maintains its melodramatic form nearly to the end.

> In melodrama we simultaneously pay homage to the idea of moral order and yet secretly enjoy the violence which threatens it. Emotionally and morally incoherent, melodrama is also blind. The tension between its overt moral ideology and its subterranean feelings goes wholly unexamined. . . . In respect of its involvement with evil, melodrama is founded upon a dialectic of gratification and repression: it partially gratifies an impulse to destruction, but at the same time, through its insistence on triumphant virtue, represses any acknowledgement of that gratification.[33]

"The dream offered by melodrama," writes Prendergast, "is . . . neither prophetic nor analytic; it is reassuring and predictable."[34]

This is precisely the sort of thing that used to be said about sentimentality in the novel. Thus Arthur Morrison, a literary naturalist who wrote melodramatic slum fiction in the 1890s, wrote with contempt about novelists who make a "public parade of sympathy," intended to allow readers to "keep their own sympathy for themselves and gain comfort from the belief that they are eased of their just responsibility by vicarious snivelling."[35] Others at the cynical fin de siècle went further

---

32. Prendergast, *Balzac*, p. 8.
33. Ibid., p. 11.
34. Ibid., p. 7.
35. Arthur Morrison, "What is a Realist?" *New Review* 16 (1897): 330.

to suggest a positive connection between sentimental self-indulgence and hard-hearted cruelty. Thus the grain of truth in Wilde's famous comment that we must have a heart of stone to read the death of Little Nell without laughing.[36]

Recently Fred Kaplan has shown that the "notion of sentimentality as insincerity, as false feeling, even as hypocrisy," is a modern prejudice, however, and that "throughout the eighteenth century and through much of the nineteenth, neither word [*sentimental* or *sentimentality*] had pejorative implication, except in special cases." Sentimentality, he explains, was a thoroughly respectable emotion, sanctified by such important eighteenth-century moral philosophers as Adam Smith and David Hume, both of whom "believed that an access of feeling cannot be an excess of feeling . . . for the basic nature of human nature is moral. . . . The more responsive we are to our moral feelings, the better, the more moral, our individual and social conduct will be."[37] Dickens, who inherited this belief from Goldsmith and others, never doubted the sincerity of sentimentalism. On the contrary, as Kaplan points out:

> Dickens believed that there is an instinctive, irrepressible need for human beings to affirm both in private and in public that they possessed moral sentiments, that these sentiments were innate, that they best expressed themselves through our spontaneous feelings, and that sentimentality in life and in art had a moral basis. People—all people, except those who have been the victims of perverse conditioning or some misfortune of nature—instinctively felt, in Dickens' view, pleasure, *moral* pleasure, when those they thought of as good triumphed and those they thought of as bad were defeated.[38]

Thus when Dickens changed the genres within his novels from melodrama to sentimental comedy, from a worldview of

---

36. Quoted in Hesketh Pearson, introduction to *Plays, Prose Writing, and Poems by Oscar Wilde* (London: J. M. Dent & Sons, 1930), p. xiii.
37. Fred Kaplan, *Sacred Tears: Sentimentality in Dickens, Thackeray, and Carlyle* (Princeton: Princeton University Press, 1987), pp. 17, 19–20.
38. Ibid., p. 3.

anger to one of love, he did not imagine that he would be perceived as ducking any issues. Anger led nowhere, or rather it led either to insignificant change or to complacent acceptance of the ruling moral order. Like the deeply wronged villain of Buckstone's famous *Luke the Labourer*, whose wife was starved to death, the melodramatic villains in Dickens from Carker the Manager and Uriah Heep to Madame Defarge and John Jasper began as the pitiful victims of a worldview they later triumphed by and that ultimately destroyed them. Luke's clenched fist became a symbol for the rage of the oppressed, but since anger was the problem, even Buckstone, let alone Dickens, knew it could hardly be the solution.

The critical books by Prendergast and Brooks that relate melodrama to such novelists as Balzac and Henry James indicate, for one thing, how closely akin this theatrical genre is to literary realism. Indeed domestic melodrama was one of the most important steps in the direction of stage realism. The plots of both melodrama and the realistic novel move through a cause-and-effect sequence toward a cul-de-sac of a despair that nineteenth-century readers found strangely comforting. The heroes and heroines of stage melodrama are illegitimately rescued through improbable hairbreadth escapes, while the central characters of realism are usually left to face consequences or swallow arsenic or throw themselves under trains, but the trap is there for all of them. The worldview dictates it inescapably.

The sensible way out of the dead end is to change the worldview, but this is not so easy a matter, since it represented the reality not only of a couple of genres but of the nineteenth century in general. This is, after all, why realism is so named. Any story about why or how things happen, which is another name for a worldview, is useful to us in the first place, as some psychologists tell us, because it seems to provide a coherent explanation for our lives. So essential is our need for coherence that we will hang onto such stories even when they do not conduce to happiness. Think, for instance, of any religious system in its last stages. The insidious aspect of a worldview is that while we possess it, or while it possesses us, it seems the only possible reality, and the most self-destructive story is apparently preferable to the chance of there being no story at all. Melodramatic realism is the fiction we currently rely on.

Just how and why the nineteenth century bought into the story of realism is irrelevant to this discussion. No doubt it was a useful fiction at some moment of deep cultural crisis. The point is that Dickens perceived it at his particular moment as crippling and suicidal. He also understood that it is the province and the obligation of the great storytellers who find themselves writing at such moments to provide us with new fictions to live by. New characters may do as well, but they must be of the sort Dickens' contemporary, Herman Melville, describes in *The Confidence-Man,* not eccentric characters, the kind Dickens was so good at creating, but truly original characters, modern archetypes, radically new conceptions of human nature, who, like revolving lights, freshly illuminate everything and everyone around them, and everything around the reader, too, thus literally providing a reconceived vision of the world.[39] Such characters are, to say the least, hard to come by. Melville, for instance, never succeeded in imagining a new Hamlet or a new Faust, only nineteenth-century versions of them, and so it was, perhaps, that he fell silent. Dickens didn't have the supreme imagination for it either, although he had the good sense to appropriate the pantomime Clown for serious literature and to see the world new through the eyes of Wilkins Micawber.

What Dickens also got from pantomime, and this is the point toward which the argument of this chapter has been aiming, was a pattern and a technique for changing genres and thus changing worldviews. The multigenred pantomime never really permits the audience to settle into the dogtrot of a cause-and-effect story. Like the character on the stage who is menaced by a spook, the audience must always be ready to "look out behind!" and to answer every complacent affirma-

---

39. Herman Melville, *The Confidence-Man,* chap. 44.

tion emanating from in back of the proscenium with a vociferous "Oh, no, it isn't!" Pantomime takes place in a world where physical laws have been temporarily suspended and where the audience identifies with a Clown who flouts most of the moral imperatives of the old story, the one the audience believed in as the only story when out in the street just a few moments before. Once the curtain goes up, the old story loses much of its grip.

Pantomime, once more, is like carnival, which, as Michael D. Bristol has described it, was "the occasion for masquerade, disguise and processions, often featuring role-reversal, gender-switching, together with special performance activities featuring both topical dramas and traditional narratives."[40] Like carnival, Dickens and pantomime are associated with traditional holiday times of the year, but they do not serve tradition. They make us feel good at the conclusion, but their vision is far from conservative. Their function, as I have said, is to provide the anarchical holiday space that Bakhtin saw as essential for the rethinking of ingrained moral and political systems and that Dickens perceived as an opportunity for changing his readers' basic stories about the nature of reality.

Transformation was the essence of pantomime—the transformation of scenery when touched by Harlequin's bat, the transformation of character and genre when touched by the Benevolent Agent's magic wand, and the Grand Transformation scenes that taxed the ingenuity of some of the greatest scenic designers of theatrical history. Martin Meisel writes:

> Paradise in the nineteenth-century theater . . . was to be found in pantomime, fairy-play, and extravaganza, that cluster of related forms. . . . A pantomime [often] began in hell . . . the cave or the grim abode of some malevolent spirit . . . but a grim opening and a dark scene, and the garish malevolence of a horde of imps and demons, served to set off the paradisal

---

40. Michael D. Bristol, *Carnival and Theater; Plebeian Culture and the Structure of Authority in Renaissance England* (New York and London: Methuen, 1985), p. 40.

character of what everyone knew was to come and had come to see, whose climactic visual achievement became the underlying rationale of the form.[41]

An unidentified article in Dickens' *All the Year Round* confirms Meisel's statement about pantomime and paradise. The writer of "Harlequin Fairy Morgana!" recalls a pantomime he saw as a child: "Once before I had been taken to this splendid spectacle; and though then of very tender years and with sensibilities scarcely developed, the impression left had been something so exquisitely unearthly, so paradisal, that I never could look back to it without an uneasy feeling reaching nearly to pain."[42] Writing in 1881, Percy Fitzgerald describes such a theatrical moment:

> All will recall in some elaborate transformation scene how quietly and gradually it evolved. First the "gauzes" lift slowly one behind the other—perhaps the most pleasing of all scenic effects—giving glimpses of "the Realms of Bliss," seen beyond in a tantalising fashion. Then is revealed a kind of half-glorified country, clouds and banks, evidently concealing much. Always a sort of pathetic and at the same time exultant strain rises, and is repeated as the changes go on. Now we hear the faint tinkle—signal to those aloft on "bridges" to open more glories. Now some of the banks begin to part slowly, showing realms of light, with a few divine beings—fairies—rising slowly here and there. More breaks beyond and fairies rising, with a pyramid of these ladies beginning to mount slowly in the centre. Thus it goes on, the lights streaming on full, in every colour and in every quarter, in the richest effulgence. In some of the more daring efforts, the *femmes suspendues* seem to float in the air or rest on the frail support of strays or branches of trees. While finally, perhaps, at the back of all, the most glorious paradise of all will open, revealing the pure empyrean itself, and some fair spirit aloft in a cloud among the stars, the apex of all.[43]

---

41. Meisel, *Realizations*, p. 184.
42. "Harlequin Fairy Morgana!" *All the Year Round* 12 (1864): 41–42. A similar article is called "Paradise Revisited," *AYR* 15 (1866): 30–34. A friend of mine, a Joyce scholar seeking information about pantomime, once asked an English acquaintance to tell her what the transformation scene is. "That's when everyone says, 'Ah!'," was the explanation.
43. Percy Fitzgerald, from *The World behind the Scenes* (New York: Benjamin Blom, 1972), p. 89.

F. Bernard, "My Last Pantomime—When I Took My Grandchildren to Covent Garden," from the *Illustrated London News*, December 23, 1876.

This is all stage magic, of course, and done with mirrors, so to speak. Unless you are there to witness the transformation, it will perhaps sound like mindless escapism. If you are a part of the audience, however, it may feel like a genuine return.

On a less metaphysical level, and considering only the two main parts of the nineteenth-century pantomime, one can say that the Opening is ruled by the power of money, thus presenting a melodramatic worldview. It makes an angry social statement, but its rage is impotent. The harlequinade, the comic business, on the other hand, is ruled by the power of sex, sex both as love and as appetite. Its worldview is comically sentimental, in the way Kaplan defines that term, and it understands itself as possessing the power to heal. And this is the way I think Frye understands the purpose behind what he calls the "freewheeling and anarchistic social outlook" of Dickens, which distinguishes his works from those of his major contemporaries:

> In most of the best Victorian novels, apart from Dickens, the society described is organized by its institutions: the church, the government, the professions, the rural squirearchy, business, and the trade unions. It is a highly structured society, and the characters function from within those structures. But in Dickens . . . the structures of society, as structures, belong almost entirely to the absurd, obsessed, sinister aspect of it, the aspect that is overcome or evaded by the comic action. The comic action itself moves toward the regrouping of society around the only social unit Dickens really regards as genuine, the family. In other Victorian novelists characters are regrouped within their social structures; in Dickens the comic action leads to a sense of having broken down or through those structures.[44]

As a result:

> The hidden world is thus, once again in literature, the world of an invincible Eros, the power strong enough to force a happy ending on the story in defiance of all probability, pushing all the obstructing humors out of the way, or killing them if they will not get out of the way, getting the attractive young people

---

44. Frye, "Dickens and the Comedy of Humors," p. 63.

disentangled from their brothers and sisters and headed for the right beds. It dissolves all hardening social institutions and reconstitutes society on its sexual basis of the family, the shadowy old fathers and mothers being replaced by new and livelier successors.[45]

The pantomime sets up one genre in order to move on to another. Dickens appropriated this structure not to give each of the genres equal weight so that they might cancel one another out but clearly to privilege the concluding vision. Thus the Dickens novel proceeds in a multitude of genres in order to create the anarchy necessary to facilitate the ultimate shift and to effect a change of heart in the reader. This was the pattern Dickens appropriated from pantomime, his plan for moral action that Orwell failed to perceive. But the structure of pantomime merely sets the stage for such transformations. In order to bring about the change Dickens looked for inspiration to a pair of pantomime characters, the Benevolent Agent and the Clown, the first of whom I shall consider in the following chapter.

45. Ibid., p. 79.

3

The Benevolent Agent and Her Pious Fraud

> "Without their visits," said the Ghost, "you cannot hope to shun the path I tread. Expect the first tomorrow, when the bell tolls one."
>
> "Couldn't I take 'em all at once, and have it over, Jacob?" hinted Scrooge.
>
> "Expect the second. . . ."

The most apparent genre transformation in Dickens takes place around the juncture between the first and second quarters of *David Copperfield*, the work that will receive most of my attention during the remainder of this study. The last chapter of the fifth monthly number is entitled "I Make Another Beginning," and the first chapter of the sixth, in which David begins his education at Doctor Strong's, is called "I am a New Boy in More Senses than One." Most readers have felt—and some of them with considerable sadness—that *David Copperfield* becomes a markedly different novel at this point.

The transformation, which involves not only a change in the direction of the plot but also in the personality of the central character and perhaps even in his sex, is accomplished by David's Aunt Betsey Trotwood. In the first chapter of the novel she had appeared as a self-appointed godmother, prepared against any and all opposition to name the expected child Betsey Trotwood Copperfield. When she was told that a boy had been born, Betsey struck the startled doctor with her purse, which was the closest thing to a wand she had about her person. Then she dematerialized. Now Betsey reappears, eccentric, but in more substantial and realistic form, to "Make

Up Her Mind About" David and to rename him Trotwood. In fact she makes most things happen for David throughout the remainder of the novel, for she is derived from the Benevolent Agent, the supernatural figure from the pantomime, who touches the characters with her magic wand near the beginning of the evening to change their natures and bring on the harlequinade and who appears again toward the end to effect the Grand Transformation, the return to paradise.

The Benevolent Agent was a formidable character in the early nineteenth century. Since there is no longer a harlequinade in the modern pantomime, and consequently no transformation of characters, she has lost most of her power. She still has the task of looking out for the young people by setting herself against the powers of evil, but she is usually not very effective anymore even in this diminished role. In a recent production of *Hansel and Gretel*, for instance, she makes such a botch of her rescues that she is ashamed to reappear on stage for a curtain call until the children, who have saved themselves, induce the audience to clap for her as if for an ailing Tinkerbell.[1]

Nowadays the part is usually played by an older, sometimes quite elderly, actress, whose quavering voice exudes grandmotherly love; but in the Regency pantomime, hers was the part of the Dame, the old woman played by an ugly man. The Dame is still played by a man in today's pantomime, the principal actor, in fact. She/he is no longer a Benevolent Agent, however, but an exuberant middle-aged woman, extravagantly dressed, large-busted, and bawdy. "I just saved a young man from being sexually attacked," says the actor playing the Dame in a 1985 production. "How did you do that?" asks the straight man. "I restrained myself."

In the early nineteenth century the sexual magic present when a man plays a woman on the British stage belonged to the Benevolent Agent. She also derived magic from her fairy-tale or nursery-rhyme origins. The mannish Betsey Trot-

---

1. At the Theatre Royal, Stratford East, December 1985.

Samuel Simmons as Mother Goose in *Harlequin and Mother Goose*, 1806. Courtesy of David Mayer III.

wood, whose name comes from the nursery-rhyme and pantomime character Dame Trot, is perhaps the most successful adaptation of the Benevolent Agent into the realm of fiction.[2] In light of the generally negative response to Dickens' first attempt(s) at this character, the Cheeryble Brothers of *Nicholas Nickleby*, it is remarkable that Betsey is the most universally admired of the personages in *David Copperfield*.

Critics of all schools find her admirable. Michael Slater calls her "the finest flowering of Dickens's concentration on women in the novels of his mid-career," and Stephen L. Franklin places her "at the moral center of the novel."[3] Sylvère Monod, who notes that David's aunt "has sometimes been regarded as the real heroine of the novel," feels that "she is at any rate its most powerful creation." Monod states that Betsey "is all that the novelist loved most: superficially eccentric and arbitrary, but at bottom generous and sensitive." Her presence in *David Copperfield* is "the supreme achievement of Dickens' art in his autobiographical novel."[4] That Dickens placed great importance upon this character is evidenced by his giving her equal billing with his hero in one of his trial titles: *"Mag's Diversions." Being the personal history, adventures, experience, and observation, of Mr David Copperfield the Younger And his Great-Aunt Margaret.*

Two important critics value Betsey from the standpoint of

---

2. A trot is an old woman or an old hag, and Dame Trot was a kind of Mother Hubbard with a comical cat instead of a dog. Nursery rhymes concerning her were printed as early as 1800. She has enjoyed a long life as a pantomime Benevolent Agent and Dame; she was Jack's mother, for instance, in John Morley's version of *Jack and the Beanstalk*, performed at Bath in 1985–86. Dickens used the name frequently in works other than *David Copperfield*: Dame Trot is one of Esther Summerson's nicknames; there are also Job Trotter and Trotty Veck, and a trot is Mr. Boffin's most usual form of locomotion.

3. Michael Slater, *Dickens and Women* (London: J. M. Dent and Sons, 1983), p. 275. Franklin says she "strikes the keynote" of *David Copperfield* as elegy when she says, "It is in vain, Trot, to recall the past, unless it works some influence upon the present." Stephen L. Franklin, "Dickens and Time: The Clock Without Hands," *Dickens Studies Annual* 4 (1975): 18–19.

4. Sylvère Monod, *Dickens the Novelist* (Norman: University of Oklahoma Press, 1968), pp. 333, 335.

realism. Q. D. Leavis discusses her as "a very human case history" on which Dickens worked "very hard."[5] Gwendolyn Needham sees her as the first of the novel's characters who succeeds in the necessary business of opening a heart, her own, that a mistaken and crippling marriage had at first closed to all mankind.[6] According to these interpretations, Betsey is a fully realistic character, subject, like David and the others, to the vicissitudes of experience. In contrast Chesterton insists that "Dickens writes realism" in the case of Betsey Trotwood only "in order to make the incredible credible."[7] A number of critics go further and have mounted formidable arguments for seeing her as David's fairy godmother, endowed with magical powers both to console and transform.[8] In direct opposition to Needham's position, A.O.J. Cockshut goes so far as to say—too far, it seems to me—that "she has no human need to conform herself to reality."[9] And, as Mrs. Leavis herself comes near to conceding,[10] there is good reason to regard David's aunt as at least a quasi-supernatural character. She appears and disappears abruptly, she lives like a witch at the edge of a cliff, and she seems to have the mystical power, twice employed in the novel, of projecting herself out of her quietly sitting body and across rooms so that she can console with a gentle touch of the hand.

Both the real and the fantastic natures of this single character are appropriate to *David Copperfield*, which is at once an English novel of development (the form that eventually

---

5. Q. D. Leavis, "Dickens and Tolstoy: The Case for a Serious View of *David Copperfield*," in *Dickens the Novelist*, by F. R. Leavis and Q. D. Leavis (London: Chatto and Windus, 1970), p. 61.
6. Gwendolyn Needham, "The Undisciplined Heart of *David Copperfield*," *Nineteenth-Century Fiction* 9 (1954): 88.
7. G. K. Chesterton, *The Victorian Age in Literature* (New York: Henry Holt, 1913), p. 125.
8. See, for instance, Shirley Grob, "Dickens and Some Motifs of the Fairy Tale," *Texas Studies in Literature and Language* 5 (1964): 570–71; and Harry Stone, *Dickens and the Invisible World: Fairy-tale, Fantasy and Novel Making* (Bloomington: Indiana University Press, 1979), pp. 197–99.
9. Cockshut, *The Imagination of Charles Dickens*, p. 121.
10. Q. D. Leavis, "Dickens and Tolstoy," pp. 90–91.

evolved into the realistic novel) and the more mystical German *Bildungsroman*. David has two distinct lessons to learn before he can achieve maturity, one Fieldingesque and the other Goethean. He must become, as Aunt Betsey tells him, "A fine firm fellow with a will of your own. With resolution. . . . With determination. . . . With strength of character that is not to be influenced except on good reason, by anybody or by anything" (pp. 234–35). This is the lesson that the hero of the English realistic novel beginning with *Tom Jones* has always to learn. But David has also a course of study set for him by Annie Strong much later in the novel: He must learn to achieve what Annie calls a disciplined heart.

Many readers have conflated these two endeavors, mistaking the second for a mere restatement of the first, but that there is a difference should be apparent from the fact that David continues to refer to his heart as undisciplined (pp. 658, 697) long after he has come to regard himself as a man of confirmed patience and perseverance (p. 517). Disciplining the heart, as David finally explains with reference to Agnes Wickfield, consists in the ability to love without any expectation of personal gratification. "I was to discipline my heart, and do my duty to her" (p. 719), David writes before getting up the strength to declare to Agnes that his love for her is selfless and disinterested (p. 737). Disciplining the heart then has nothing to do with Fielding and his perhaps overly generous hero. It is a species of renunciation that Dickens probably learned from Carlyle's translation of the archetypical German *Bildungsroman*, Goethe's *Wilhelm Meister*. Indeed, Richard Dunn has written that *David Copperfield* can "be read as both an echo of and a sequel to *Sartor Resartus*" and that Carlyle, Goethe's British disciple, had meant, and Dickens had understood, the disciplining of heart to mean "renunciation of the self (that is, renunciation of selfishness)."[11]

The two distinct lessons, coming as they do from different

---

11. Richard Dunn, "David Copperfield's Carlylean Retailoring," in *Dickens the Craftsman: Strategies of Presentation*, ed. Robert B. Partlow, Jr. (Carbondale: Southern Illinois University Press, 1970), pp. 97, 111.

cultures and markedly different genres of fiction, seem to call for different methods of education. From as early at least as *The Magic Flute* the German lesson had been taught through an elegantly complex mystical initiation, while the English hero usually learned only through simple, hard experience, by having his face rubbed in it, so to speak. Aunt Betsey apparently intends to follow the English plan in bringing about the English maturity, the firmness of character, she wants David to achieve. She frankly points out to him that both his parents would have been the better if they had possessed greater strength of character; she sends him to a good, no-nonsense school; and she has him live away from home. When David has a hard time choosing a career, she buys him "a little breathing-time," so that he can look at the question "from a new point of view, and not as a schoolboy" (p. 234). When this plan does not produce the desired results, Betsey does not lose patience; she steps in without recriminations, finds him a good job, and sets him up in independent London lodgings. At this point, "My aunt informed me how she confidently trusted that the life I was to lead would make me firm and self-reliant, which was all I wanted" (p. 303).

This is model parenting from the English point of view—frank, caring, and trusting; but what can we say about Betsey's next move in David's education, which is to tell him that she has lost her entire fortune? The statement is based on a truth, but it is an exaggeration. In fact the statement is a lie; she still has two thousand pounds, which she had not invested with Wickfield and which Heep therefore could not make off with. Later on Betsey justifies herself, saying, "I wanted to see how you would come out of the trial, Trot" (p. 665).

Moral characters do tell lies in realistic novels—no doubt they tell them more frequently than they do in most romances—but Harry Stone is right when he calls this particular kind of falsehood "a typical folk-tale testing."[12] When such tests or constructed ordeals occur in Biblical literature,

---

12. Stone, *Dickens and the Invisible World*, p. 260.

folk tales, chivalric romances, and other romantic stories, the purpose is sometimes merely to assess the character of the person being tested. This is certainly the motive in many pantomime openings, where the Benevolent Agent seeks to learn which of the young girl's suitors she ought to befriend. Frequently, however, both in the pantomime and elsewhere such tests aim not only to measure but also to inculcate virtue; they are educational devices. In David's case the situation of his aunt's supposed poverty, together with his need to become an eligible suitor for Dora, forces him to develop the qualities Aunt Betsey has been aiming at. "You came out nobly," she tells him later (p. 665).

Betsey's falsehood has successfully formed David's character, and while there may be nothing unrealistic about a character telling a lie, the implications of the aesthetics of such an action are contrary to the realist position. A falsehood or fiction perpetrated for the child's good would therefore be out of place in a realistic novel because the very notion of education through deception cuts at the heart of the philosophy of realism, which holds that the truth only is good for us and that we learn by confronting it. Realism teaches not by misleading its characters and readers but by disillusioning them, forcing them to see the world "as it really is."

Nineteenth-century English educational theory is unequivocal in this regard, as the writings of Herbert Spencer indicate. Although Spencer appears not to have read Rousseau, he is in agreement with the author of *Emile* in believing that children should not be lied to and should not be punished when they tell lies, only be made to suffer the consequences of their untruths. Rousseau, however, is not above improving these consequences by pretending not to believe anything Emile says for some time after he tells his lie. Spencer, on the other hand, insists that any tampering with purely natural consequences will give the child a false picture of reality.[13]

---

13. See Jean-Jacques Rousseau, *Emile: or On Education*, trans. Allan Bloom (New York: Basic Books, 1979), p. 101; and Spencer's *Education; Intellectual, Moral, and Physical* (New York and London: D. Appleton, 1860), p. 182.

Aunt Betsey has gone much farther than even Rousseau, let alone Spencer, would allow, and so it appears that even the English side of David Copperfield's development is brought about through an educational technique foreign to both realism and the realistic novel. Betsey does not scruple to lie again, or as good as lie, when it is a question of completing the German part of David's education, of forcing him to go through with the harder task of disciplining his heart. In order to prove himself this time, David must be made to believe that Agnes, whom he now loves, is in love with, and about to marry, someone else. Only then can he make the requisite Goethean renunciation:

> I must speak plainly. If you have any lingering thought that I could envy the happiness you will confer; that I could not resign you to a dearer protector, of your own choosing; that I could not, from my removed place, be a contented witness of your joy; dismiss it, for I don't deserve it! I have not suffered quite in vain. You have not taught me quite in vain. There is no alloy of self in what I feel for you. (P. 737)

Agnes responds that she has loved no one but David all her life—so all ends happily—but she would never have found the opportunity to tell him so if David had not been misled by two of Aunt Betsey's intentionally equivocal speeches.

David calls his aunt's deception "a pious fraud" (p. 740). This is the same expression Bella Wilfer Harmon will use in *Our Mutual Friend* to describe Mr. Boffin's much more elaborate fiction in pretending to have become a miser in order to provide her with a "glaring instance" of her own mercenary proclivities. It also describes a number of deceptions elsewhere in Dickens, perpetrated either by characters to benefit other characters or by the author to benefit his readers. Dickens, however, did not coin the term *pious fraud*. Victorians used it to denote any falsehood told with a moral motive.[14] The *OED*, however, lists an eighteenth-century usage

---

14. Dickens used the term in a letter to Thomas Beard, 18 December 1842, in which he plots to use Beard as a fictitious buyer of a painting by Maclise,

that is strikingly relevant to Dickens' practice, especially in his earlier works: In a *Spectator* paper of 1712, Addison, in discussing the fantastic, noted that "the Ancients have not much of this Poetry among them; for, indeed, almost the whole Substance of it owes its Original to the Darkness and Superstition of later Ages, when pious Frauds were made use of to amuse Mankind and frighten them into a Sense of their Duty."[15]

So understood, pious frauds involving fear, the supernatural, and a moral lesson had been the modus operandi of a great deal of Dickens' shorter fiction from as early as "The Story of the Goblin Who Stole a Sexton" from *Pickwick Papers* and continuing through the first two of the Christmas Books, *A Christmas Carol* and *The Chimes*, which is subtitled *A Goblin Story*. The fraud becomes more domestic but no less pious in *The Cricket on the Hearth: A Fairy Tale of the Home*, where the Benevolent Agent reassures rather than frightens. Beginning with *The Battle of Life* (1846), the deceptions sometimes operate without the help of the overtly supernatural, although Benevolent Agents like John Jarndyce, Noddy Boffin, and Betsey Trotwood are realistic characters only when we take strict care not to look away from them for a single moment.

Critics with realist orientations have frequently found these devices insulting. Thus in 1858 J. C. Jeaffreson called Dickens "as deceitful, deceiving, and wittingly dishonest a describer as can be found in the entire range of living authors."[16] In our own generation Robert Garis complained that

---

who would not accept money from Dickens because of their friendship. *The Letters of Charles Dickens* (Oxford: Clarendon Press, 1974), 3: 396. In *No Name*, Wilkie Collins uses the term to denote merely a harmless deception. *Works* (New York: Peter Fenelon Collier, n.d.), 13: 45–46.

15. Number 419, 1 July 1712, *The Spectator* (London: J. and R. Tonson and S. Draper, 1753), 6: 95.

16. J. C. Jeaffreson, *Novels and Novelists, from Elizabeth to Victoria* (London: Hurst and Blacklett, 1858), 2: 273. Even earlier, Edgar Allen Poe had respectfully complained of Dickens' "disingenuous and inartistical . . . oversight" of referring to Barnaby Rudge's mother as the widow. *Graham's Magazine* 20 (February 1842): 126–27.

Hablot Browne, "The Goblins Who Stole a Sexton," 1836, from *Pickwick Papers*. Courtesy of the University of California at Riverside Library.

Dickens' theatrical mystification exploits rather than cures our moral stupidity.[17] Moreover, as W. D. Howells' reaction attests, realists have never found the conversions effected by these pious frauds convincing.

> People always knew that character is not changed by a dream in a series of tableaux; that a ghost cannot do much towards reforming an inordinately selfish person; that a life cannot be turned white, like a head of hair, in a single night, by the most allegorical apparition; that want and sin and shame cannot be cured by kettles singing on the hob; and gradually they ceased to make believe there was virtue in these devices and appliances.[18]

The surprising fact is that very few legitimate writers besides Dickens have *ever* felt there was any virtue in these devices. Of course deceptions take place frequently in novels of all schools, and they are the lifeblood of the theater, but *pious* frauds, where the purpose of the deception is to benefit the person being deceived, are astoundingly hard to find. They occur in Goldsmith, maybe in *The Vicar of Wakefield* and certainly, but inconsequentially, in *The Good Natured Man*.[19] They abound in Shakespeare, who was Dickens' chief influence in this regard. But pious frauds exist practically nowhere else in serious English literature.[20] It is little wonder, therefore, that the technique is so severely criticized. When, in *Our Mutual Friend*, Dickens took a cue from Shakespeare's *The Winter's Tale*, deciding to include the readers among those to be piously deceived by the Benevolent Agent, the outcry was so

---

17. Robert Garis, *The Dickens Theatre* (Oxford: Oxford University Press, 1965).

18. W. D. Howells, "Criticism and Fiction," in *Criticism and Fiction and Other Essays*, ed. Clara Marburg Kirk and Rudolf Kirk (New York: New York University Press, 1959), p. 83.

19. Interestingly Dickens thought of both Henry Fielding *and* Oliver Goldsmith as names for the son who was born just before Dickens began writing *David Copperfield*.

20. Earle Davis has discovered another pious fraud in the ultra-Shakespearean Sheridan Knowles' *The Hunchback*, which, as Davis points out, was unquestionably the source for Boffin's fraud in *Our Mutual Friend*. Davis, *The Flint and the Flame*, pp. 264–82.

great that it still reverberates.[21] "Such manipulation of people, in life or in art," writes Grahame Smith, "is at once arrogant and frivolous." The practice is, in essence, not English, and thus Smith senses in it "a failure of nerve."[22]

Despite the pious frauds of Dickens and Shakespeare, realism remained the essential mode of English art and thought. Dickens acknowledged this when, very late in his career, he defined literature from Mr. Podsnap's perspective as "large print, respectfully descriptive of getting up at eight, shaving close at a quarter past, breakfasting at nine, going to the city at ten, coming home at half-past five, and dining at seven." Although the night is left discreetly blank, there is little room in such realistic art either for Marley's ghost or the dreams of midsummer. This situation came about not only because such things were considered stuff and nonsense and therefore ill-suited to the practical English temper. The word *respectfully* carries weight in the passage just quoted from *Our Mutual Friend*, for it describes a relationship between author and reader that the English insisted on and that the nonthreatening writer of the realistic novel was usually willing enough to arrange.

No one provided it any better or more willingly than Anthony Trollope, who told his public that he became a novelist because he wasn't smart enough for anything else and who aspired no higher than to be his reader's friend or companion. Thus Trollope ruled out frauds on the reader, pious or otherwise, because "the author and the reader should move along together in full confidence with each other. Let the personages of the drama undergo ever so complete a comedy of errors among themselves, but let the spectator never mistake the Syracusan for the Ephesian. Otherwise he is one of the dupes, and the part of a dupe is never dignified."[23] The

---

21. Rosemary Mundhenk writes in "The Education of the Reader in *Our Mutual Friend*," that "Dickens does for the reader what Boffin does for Bella." *Nineteenth-Century Fiction* 34 (1979): 42.

22. Grahame Smith, *Dickens, Money, and Society* (Berkeley and Los Angeles: University of California Press, 1968), p. 183.

23. Anthony Trollope, *Barchester Towers*, chap. 15.

reader of Victorian realism wanted to be educated by the author in some particulars, and if he had a fault, he didn't really mind his friend pointing it out to him in a frank and straightforward fashion or even sometimes with a dig of affectionate irony, but he didn't expect to be tricked into changing his character or his basic view of the world. When that was attempted, the implications were that the author considered the reader not good enough to begin with and, therefore, unsuited for a respectful friendship.

No writer needed a relationship with his readers more desperately than Dickens did, and few people have ever valued friendship more highly. Nevertheless for him, novel writing was not a membership card to a gentlemen's club. Witness his castigation in *Bleak House* of those artists who gain their invitations to Chesney Wold by respectfully "walking backward like the Lord Chamberlain" (chap. 12, p. 160). Art was a profession and a calling. As Carlyle had insisted, it entailed serious, even priestly responsibilities. Unlike Trollope, Dickens did not suppose he had become a novelist because he could not do anything else; on the contrary, he thought he could have done anything superlatively well. And if the praise of shorthand reporters and theatrical people and connoisseurs of public speaking counts for anything, he seems to have been right about himself. Living in the midst of the most genteelly unassuming set of writers even England has produced,[24] he never pretended to be anything less than a genius, "the inimitable," and he criticized fellow writers when, according to his lights, they pretended to modesty or to be doing inconsequential work. Thackeray often said, as he once wrote to Trollope, "I am like the pastry-cook, and don't care for tarts, but prefer bread and cheese; but the public love tarts (luckily for us), and we must bake and sell them."[25] Dickens

---

24. Bradford Booth writes that "the Victorian novelist did not take himself very seriously. Since he wrote for a disparate, heterogeneous group and aimed primarily at amusement, he did not often assume the mantle of the poet or the prophet." *Anthony Trollope: Aspects of His Life and Art* (Bloomington: Indiana University Press, 1958), p. 23.

25. 28 October 1859. *The Letters and Private Papers of William Makepeace*

would have none of this authorial cult snobbery. He once wrote to Bulwer-Lytton his conviction "that the audience is good enough for anything that is well presented to it."[26] Dickens knew Thackeray's attitude, and even when he wrote an obituary tribute about his great rival, he felt constrained to scold him for feigning "a want of earnestness" and for making "a pretence of undervaluing his art, which was not good for the art that he held in trust."[27]

I am not convinced that Dickens' art, based as it was on the manipulation of characters and readers, was more arrogant, as we have heard one critic imply, than the art of the realists, and I am quite certain that there was nothing frivolous about his use of the pious fraud. That readers take umbrage at such usage and at his depiction of them in his portraits of the heroes and heroines with whom he expects them to identify, is understandable. But it is best to remember that we are not in polite society when we read Dickens. He was not in the business of flattering his readers' egos but of changing their bad, self-destructive stories about themselves and the world. He had enough respect for his readers to believe they were capable of being changed, but he knew they were not going to let him do it with straight, rational talk, for it was precisely such talk, according to his lights, that had permitted the bad stories to take hold in the first place. England was in the sorry state in which he had found it because of an undue respect for rational, unimaginative, inoffensive behavior compounded by an incoherent hankering after gentility. What was required, therefore, was pantomime magic—trickery and artistic illusion—capable of providing his readers with glaring instances of their destructive worldview and of showing them

---

Thackeray, ed. Gordon N. Ray (Cambridge: Harvard University Press, 1946), 4: 158–59.

26. Letter to Lord Lytton, 20 December 1861. *The Letters of Charles Dickens*, ed. Walter Dexter (Bloomsbury: The Nonesuch Press, 1938), 3: 255.

27. Charles Dickens, "In Memoriam: W. M. Thackeray," *Cornhill Magazine*, February 1864. Reprinted in *Collected Papers* (Bloomsbury: The Nonesuch Press, 1938), 1: 98.

the possibility of a better vision with a concluding pantomime Grand Transformation to paradise and the lost green world.

The first transformation in *David Copperfield*, as I began this chapter by saying, occurs at the juncture of the first and second quarters of the novel. And it is in the sixth monthly number when David becomes "a New Boy in More Senses than One" that the first significant pious fraud of the story begins. Many of the characters, including the narrator, and all of the readers are made to believe that Annie Strong, the wife of David's schoolmaster, is in love with her worthless cousin Jack Maldon and in danger of being seduced by him. This story is continued in the seventh number and then largely suspended until the fourteenth and fifteenth, that is to say, until the conclusion of what I have previously called the quarter of serious melodrama, the point in the novel at which Dickens typically transforms a world of hate, suspicion, and resentment into one of comedy, love, and sentiment. In the fifteenth number, in a grand, melodramatic scene, Annie tells all of us, characters and readers alike, that she had got over her childish infatuation long before her first appearance in the novel and that for years, during the very time Dickens encouraged us to tremble for her, she had refused even to speak with her cousin except in public.

That readers as well as characters have been taken in by this deception is evidenced by the confusion of the estimable Dickens scholar Earle Davis, who later became one of the most perceptive critics of Dickens' pious frauds:

> Perhaps it is Dickens's point that Annie should not have encouraged Jack Maldon at all. His intent in the story is not clear, I think. As the earlier scenes are presented, and Mr. Wickfield gets Maldon away to India on an appointment, I felt that it was all a fine interpretation of a girl in a difficult situation, admiring and loving her elderly husband, and fighting a passion which she really knows to be wrong. But this interpretation is ruined by the denouement which comes later in the story. From the conclusion, the reader is asked to believe that she never even thought of loving Maldon—a conclusion which is hard to accept when one sees her on her knees looking up at

the old doctor on the night after Maldon has departed for India.[28]

This somewhat puzzled reaction interestingly parallels Grahame Smith's attack on the Boffin fraud. Smith ended, as we have seen, by denouncing Dickens' arrogant and frivolous manipulation of people and by sensing in the author "a failure of nerve." Earlier he wrote:

> Boffin belongs to the tradition of Dickens' genially eccentric old benefactors, and yet we feel convinced that Dickens is prepared to sacrifice him in the interests of artistic truth. His failure to do so is damaging . . . to the entire novel, but it makes nonsense of the earlier stages in which we have watched Boffin's breakdown. . . . It cannot be denied that the weakness of the Boffin strand seriously undermines the novel's artistic unity.[29]

Readers have been far less upset over the Annie Strong fraud because Dickens manages it without a Benevolent Agent within the story and because the narrator, David Copperfield, is as badly fooled as anyone else. It is also a much less compelling deception than the one involving Boffin, so the reader cares less about it. But it is no less a fraud, and it is certainly no less important to the meaning of the novel in which it appears.

This last statement requires some explanation, for the Annie Strong story has generally been regarded as one of the weaker, if not less significant, of the several subplots in *David Copperfield*. The Annie Strong plot is related to the plot of Shakespeare's *The Winter's Tale* not simply by the presence in each of a pious fraud on both characters and readers. The two stories confront the philosophical problem of skepticism as exemplified by the loss of faith in a pure woman's chastity. Once again, both writers were working against the realistic current of their times. Dickens had the worldly wisdom of university men like Thackeray to contend with. Shakespeare,

---

28. Earle Davis, "The Creation of Dickens's *David Copperfield:* A Study in Narrative Craft," *Bulletin: Municipal University of Wichita* 16 (1941): 21.
29. Smith, *Dickens, Money, and Society*, pp. 182–83.

although unwilling to admit impediments to the marriage of true minds, must have known that his lesser but more representative and more intellectually respectable contemporaries, educated men like John Donne, were ready enough to "Swear, / No where, / Lives a woman true and fair."

As the philosopher Stanley Cavell points out, Shakespeare had tried to deal with this same problem in *Othello*, where it had proved unsolvable. Skepticism is the result of too much knowledge, and the genre of Renaissance tragedy, as Cavell perceptively defines it, is itself "the outcome of the problem of knowledge . . . the dominance of modern philosophical thought by it."[30] Once faith is lost—once Othello ceases to believe in Desdemona's chastity or Leontes in Hermione's—it is beyond what Cavell terms the claim of reason, the province of rational, philosophical thought, to call it back. Thus tragedy fails as a genre to defeat skepticism, and the Moor dies. But the romance of *The Winter's Tale* with its imaginative and artistic deceptions—the living statue of Hermione and Paulina's false story of her death—succeeds in restoring Leontes' belief in his wife, in the world, and, most importantly, perhaps, in himself.

Faith in the purity of good women, emblematic of faith in the goodness of human nature, is as central to *David Copperfield* as it is to *Othello*. "My life upon her faith!" the Moor says of Desdemona, but it is really *his* faith that is at issue. And so it is with David Copperfield, who must ultimately depend on Agnes Wickfield to rescue him from his paralyzing fear of death and whose faith in her inviolability is threatened during these chapters by the rise of Uriah Heep. The grief-stricken Mr. Wickfield, whose life also depends on the purity of his daughter and whose radical distrust of human nature is the novel's most dangerous disease, ironically fears the infection that might spread from the suspected Annie Strong. In Wickfield's grief-stricken mind, which he ultimately acknowledges as diseased, Annie seems to pose a threat to the purity

---

30. Stanley Cavell, *The Claim of Reason: Wittgenstein, Skepticism, Morality, and Tragedy* (Oxford: Oxford University Press, 1979), p. 482.

of Agnes. Thus he dislikes the intimacy between Annie and his daughter. And David, catching Wickfield's distrustfulness, confesses that "the innocent beauty of [Annie's] face was not so innocent to me as it had been; I mistrusted the natural grace and charm of her manner, and when I looked at Agnes at her side, and thought how good and true Agnes was, suspicion arose within me that it was an ill-assorted friendship" (p. 19). With his doubt of Annie Strong, which includes a want of perfect faith in Agnes, her friend, the novel's universe rocks on foundations that had already been weakened in the tenth number when Little Em'ly fell to Steerforth. "If she be false," as Othello says, "O, then heaven mocks itself!" "O Agnes," David begins the last sentence of the novel, "O my soul."

But, of course, Agnes is not false, and neither is Annie Strong. The fraud that made us conclude that Annie was unfaithful, like the deceptions practiced by the spirits of Christmas and the goblins of the chimes, and like the elaborate fiction of Boffin in *Our Mutual Friend*, was intended only to make us see the inevitable consequences of the worldview Dickens wants us to abandon. This purpose accomplished, Dickens exposes his fraud, and he does so in the fifteenth number, at precisely the spot in all the late novels where, after giving us our darkest moment, Dickens lets in the ray of light that is to expand and illuminate the comedy of the last five numbers. With the help of the Benevolent Agent, Aunt Betsey (who mutters parenthetically throughout the scene to prevent the interruptions of Annie's malevolent mother), and at the instigation of Betsey's protegé, Mr. Dick, Annie not only vindicates herself but sounds the keynote of the concept of the disciplined heart, which is ultimately to win Agnes for David. In the chapter after the conclusion of this fraud, as the Dickens world begins to steady itself, David even learns that the supposedly lost Emily has run away from Steerforth and will perhaps be saved as well.

There follow now the three great comic and sentimental climaxes of *David Copperfield*, the explosion of Heep and the deaths of Dora and Steerforth. And then in the final number comes the ultimate pious fraud of the novel, Aunt Betsey's disingenuous suggestions that Agnes is about to be married. The purpose here is to force David to prove that he has finally learned the truth that Annie Strong enunciated at the moment of her vindication when she thanked her husband for having saved her "from the first mistaken impulses of my undisciplined heart" (p. 564).

Disciplining the heart, as I argued earlier in this chapter, is the lesson of David's German *Bildung,* and it is not only the concept that was derived from *Wilhelm Meister* but also the method of teaching it. We have seen that pious frauds, especially those in which the reader or audience is deceived along with the characters, are extremely rare in serious literature. Indeed, one of the few I have been able to discover outside of Dickens and Shakespeare occurs toward the end of the *Lehrjahre* when Wilhelm is taught the same lesson of renunciation that David has to master before he can win Agnes and become the hero of his own life.

Wilhelm lived within a community of friends, all of whom patiently dedicate themselves to the task of bringing him to maturity, and since *Wilhelm Meister* is a German *Bildungsroman* and not an English novel of development, Wilhelm's friends do not scruple to proceed in a less than straightforward manner. I do not suppose that Goethe ever worried, as Trollope did, about qualifying as his reader's trusted friend. After a number of purely impulsive love affairs, Wilhelm is educated by his friends to the point of proposing to Theresa, one of the novel's heroines. It is a rational decision. As Wilhelm rather awkwardly says, at least in Carlyle's shaky translation, which must have been Dickens' source, "This resolution, of soliciting Theresa's hand, is probably the first that has proceeded altogether from myself. I laid my plan considerately; my reason fully joined in it; by the consent of that noble maiden all my hopes were crowned."[31] But things are never this simple in Goethe, for, as in *David Copperfield*, rational maturity is not

---

31. Johann Wolfgang von Goethe, *Wilhelm Meister,* trans. Thomas Carlyle (London, 1824), book 8, chap. 4.

enough. Before she met Wilhelm, Theresa had been about to marry Lothario, Wilhelm's valued friend, but the engagement ended when it was discovered that the lovers were apparently brother and sister. Now it is just as suddenly reported that they are not related after all. Theresa, who still loves Lothario, fears some kind of trick and presses for an early marriage with Wilhelm, who is in a constant state of ill-humor during these chapters because he suspects, and with good reason, that people are playing games with his life, perhaps for his own good but maybe arrogantly and frivolously. Nevertheless he decides that Lothario "well merits every sort of friendship and affection" and that "without sacrifices, friendship cannot be imagined."[32] Thus for Lothario's sake Wilhelm renounces his bride.

Goethe almost certainly intended some irony in this episode, for Wilhelm is already beginning to half suspect, when he makes his grand sacrifice, that he is falling in love with a more suitable woman. Still the exercise appears to have accomplished the hero's *Bildung*, and the irony seems anyway to have been lost on Carlyle and also on Dickens, who in 1846 had written a Christmas Book, *The Battle of Life*, in which two noble sisters, both in love with the same man, vie to outdo one another in the business of renunciation. *The Battle of Life* is Dickens' most Goethean work, and it contains one of the most arrant of Dickens' pious frauds on the reader.[33]

Thus the pious frauds of *David Copperfield* are related thematically to the novel's core and are warranted aesthetically by Shakespeare and Goethe, the two writers whom Dickens would have been taught to revere as the most intellectually

32. Ibid.
33. The characters and the readers are made to believe that the sister whom the young man favors has run off with a lover. In this case, Dickens was materially aided by one of his illustrators, John Leech, who obviously did not read to the conclusion and produced an illustration documenting the elopement, which, of course, never took place. Dickens discovered the mistake in time to prevent its publication, but decided not to, out of fear, so he said, of embarrassing poor Leech. See Forster, *Life of Charles Dickens*, pp. 439–40.

significant of his story-telling precursors. Dickens seldom justifies the value of art with reference to its great masters, however. When Shakespeare's plays are performed in his novels, it is usually in laughable productions by Crummles and Waldengarver. David Copperfield is highly impressed by the Covent Garden *Julius Caesar,* but, as Steerforth tells him, "There never was a more miserable business" (p. 246). More frequently the claim of art is made by Dickens in terms of Astley's Horse Riding and Sleary's Circus and Mrs. Jarley's waxworks. A so-called serious artist like Henry Gowan has no values to impart, whereas the miniaturist Miss La Creevy fills *Nicholas Nickleby* with the idealism her small art unconsciously parodies.

It is the same with the pious fraud. Dickens recognized it in Shakespeare and Goethe, but he also saw it in popular fairy tales and in the pantomime, where the fairy tales were given theatrical life. One fairy-tale pious fraud that I will discuss when I consider Little Em'ly's incoherent compulsion to be a lady is the motif of the bad wish fulfilled, in which, as frequently employed by Dickens, a Benevolent Spirit realizes a character's questionable desires, like Pip's great expectations or Little Dorrit's dream to see her father free, in order that they and we can learn to wish more responsibly. Another is the expiatory harlequinade, which in some pantomimes is imposed by the Benevolent Agent as a means of permitting a faulty pair of lovers to redeem themselves by undergoing the trials of Harlequin and Columbine.[34] I shall glance at some of these later on when I consider the faulty heroes of Dickens and of the pantomime. But the antirealistic harlequinade is always a pious fraud on the characters; its effect, moreover, is to redeem even the worst of them and to redeem the audience as well.

In Dickens, as opposed to the pantomime, this effect is the aim of a conscious aesthetic. Dickens' Benevolent Agents—the Cheerybles, Aunt Betsey, John Jarndyce, Mr. Boffin,

---

34. See chap. 6, pp. 119–20.

together with the goblins and spirits of the Christmas Books —have the task of teaching both characters and audiences that they are better than they think they are. Usually they do this by convincing us through magical sleight of hand that the life stories we have come to credit are both false and self-destructive, thus clearing a carnivalesque space for nobler conceptions of ourselves and the world and preparing a stage for the Clown, who may ultimately redeem us.

But before confronting the Clown in the final chapters of this study, I will consider more closely the rest of the dramatis personae of the Dickens pantomime in order to explain the specifics of the worldview from which Dickens believed his contemporaries needed to be rescued. In the succeeding chapters we shall discover that what Andrew Halliday called "the simple story of Clown, Pantaloon, Harlequin, and Columbine" could have sinister and culturally significant implications when adopted by the imagination of Charles Dickens.

4

Pantaloon: Some Dickensian Parents

> I will give you a piece of Patriarchal advice—Don't have any more children. If the childless kings and queens in the stories had only known what they were about, they would never have bothered the Fairies to give them families.
> —Dickens to Mrs. Lehmann

> The pantalooning work takes the pride and spirit out of a man.
> —Andrew Halliday

Dickens began with very mixed reactions to Pantaloon. In 1837 when he was writing his first piece on the pantomime, he regarded this conventional bad father as "of all the pantomimic *dramatis personae* . . . the most worthless and debauched. . . . a treacherous worldly-minded old villain."[1] Yet the next year, when he was editing the *Memoirs of Joseph Grimaldi*, a book that has more interesting things to say about good and bad parenting than about the theater, Dickens recalled his childhood wish that "Pantaloon were our godfather."[2] Such ambivalent feelings are understandable in a young man, especially if his father is John Dickens; they are also understandable in terms of the pantomime itself. All the characters in the harlequinade give mixed signals, but none is more confusing than this mischievous old lecher, who represents patriarchal authority and the corrupt hierarchy. In the opening Pantaloon is the blocking figure of New Comedy who tries to force his daughter into a loveless marriage,

---

1. Dickens, "The Pantomime of Life," p. 292.
2. Dickens, introduction to *Memoirs of Joseph Grimaldi*, p. xii.

and whom Northrop Frye characterizes as "generally cruel or foolish."[3] After his harlequinade transformation, moreover, Pantaloon's standard business in the plot is a prolonged attempt to capture the young lovers and frustrate their desires. However, with Clown's help he is quickly distracted from chasing after the tricky Harlequin and easily deflected into a series of comic adventures. It is as difficult, therefore, for an audience to work up any real dislike for him as it was for an audience of my own childhood to hate his descendant, Elmer Fudd of the Bugs Bunny cartoons.

Pantaloon's relationship with Clown is one of the most complex and confusing aspects of the comic business. Clown is Pantaloon's servant, but given his nature he acts inadvertently and sometimes consciously to sabotage the chase. Sometimes he even takes a bribe to help the young people. This is, however, only the beginning of the confusion. For the two antagonists have a comic/straight man relationship that resembles a marriage and sometimes amounts almost to a shared identity. Pantomime scenarios of the 1830s, *Harlequin and the King of Clubs,* for instance, refer to them as "Clown and his inseparable friend."[4] An article by Andrew Halliday, written for Dickens' magazine *All the Year Round,* recounts the career of one stage Pantaloon in a way that, despite the comic tone, brings out the jealousy and the intimacy of the Pantaloon narrator's association with the Clown. "I've had an awful life with Joey," writes the fictitious Pantaloon actor, "and that's the truth." In his personal life the Clown "has been a lucky dog all through," and in the harlequinade, he "always has the best of it [with the audience] however good the pantaloon may be."[5]

---

3. Frye, "Dickens and the Comedy of Humors," p. 68.

4. *Harlequin and the King of Clubs; or, the Knave who Stole the Syllabub* (Adelphi Theatre 26/12/1832). In this play there are two clowns, who are also referred to as Pantaloon's companions and associates. In *Harlequin and the Elfin Arrow; or, The Basket Maker and His Brother* (Queen's Theatre 12/12/1832), Clown is called Pantaloon's "companion" in one scene and his friend in another.

5. Andrew Halliday, "Pantaloon," *All the Year Round* 8 (13 September 1862), 10. Halliday was a regular contributor to the journal, as well as an ac-

Pantaloon, from a Juvenile Drama Sheet, circa 1830.

> The clown, don't you see, has the upper hand. . . . He makes fun of everybody, knocks everybody about, even the police, and never comes to much harm himself. This sort of character, it seems to me, always gets well through the world.

On the other hand, the narrator continues, "the pantalooning work takes the pride and spirit out of a man."[6] What is more bitter still is the reflection that the fates of the men, both on and off the stage, might easily have been reversed, for the two actors in Halliday's sketch used to alternate roles early in their partnership until a mere toss of the coin decided which of them was to play the Clown on a regular basis. Subsequently Joey married a rich widow and lived well, while the narrator became a jealous and complaining failure. "He has kicked and cuffed and battered me into what I am—a shaky old pantaloon."[7]

It was this confusion between Clown and Pantaloon that made the conception of Mr. Pickwick possible, as well as the conversion of Scrooge, and it may account for Dickens' and our own mixed-up feelings about Fagin, whom Michael Hollington sees as "a mime artist" and a combination "pantomimic buffoon, horrific sadist, mythic demon and, at the last, terrified victim."[8] This confusion may also help to explain the ambivalence perceptive readers like James R. Kincaid and Robert Polhemus have sensed in novels like *Martin Chuzzlewit*, where Pecksniff, surely one of the greatest of Dickens' Pantaloons, is villain on one page and pratfall buffoon on the next.[9] In most of the later works, starting with *Dombey and Son*, where Rob the Grinder becomes the tool of James Car-

---

tive playwright. His stage adaptations of Dickens' novels were highly regarded in their own time, and even Dickens, who almost always disliked stage adaptations of his works, enjoyed Halliday's version of *David Copperfield*.

6. Ibid., p. 12.
7. Ibid., p. 10.
8. Hollington, *Dickens and the Grotesque*, pp. 62, 64.
9. See James R. Kincaid, *Dickens and the Rhetoric of Laughter* (Oxford: Oxford University Press, 1971), pp. 150–56, and Robert Polhemus, *Comic Faith: The Great Tradition from Austen to Joyce* (Chicago: University of Chicago Press, 1980).

ker, the Clown is associated with the villain, but in some of the early novels he begins as an ally of the bad or weak father, as in the pantomime itself. In *Nicholas Nickleby,* for instance, Newman Noggs works for Uncle Ralph rather than for the wicked lover. Ralph is sufficiently villainous, but he does not himself threaten the chastity of either of the novel's heroines as Arthur Gride and Sir Mulberry Hawk do; Ralph's chief failures are as foster father to Nicholas and Kate and as father to Smike. His exploitation of Kate causes him to feel a powerful though temporary twinge of conscience, and his neglect of Smike, when he learns of it, drives him to his suicide. Pecksniff is even more confusing, perhaps, because he is both a father whose schemes result in a tragic marriage for his daughter and the would-be wicked lover of Mary Graham. But it is only when he reveals himself in this second role that the Clown, Tom Pinch, parts company with him. It has been a significant association: "'You left Mr. Pecksniff!' cried the tollman, folding his arms, and spreading his legs. 'I should as soon have thought of his head leaving him'" (chap. 31, p. 502). To complicate matters even more, since the father figure in the pantomime had amorous propensities, which Dickens found reprehensible,[10] such unsuitable lovers as Arthur Gride of *Nicholas Nickleby* tend sometimes to resemble the stage Pantaloon:

> The person who made this reply was a little old man, of about seventy or seventy-five years of age, of a very lean figure, much bent, and slightly twisted. He wore a grey coat with a very narrow collar, and old-fashioned waistcoat of ribbed black silk, and such scanty trousers as displayed his shrunken spindle-shanks in their full ugliness. The only articles of display or ornament in his dress were a steel watch-chain to

---

10. In "The Pantomime of Life" Dickens wrote, "His amorous propensities . . . are eminently disagreeable; and his mode of addressing ladies in the open street at noon-day is downright improper, being usually neither more nor less than a perceptible tickling of the aforesaid ladies in the waist, after committing which, he starts back, manifestly ashamed (as well he may be) of his own indecorum and temerity; continuing, nevertheless, to ogle and beckon to them from a distance in a very unpleasant and immoral manner" (p. 292).

which were attached some large gold seals; and a black ribbon into which, in compliance with an old fashion scarcely ever observed in these days, his grey hair was gathered behind. His nose and chin were sharp and prominent, his jaws had fallen inwards from loss of teeth, his face was shrivelled and yellow, save where the cheeks were streaked with the colour of a dry winter apple; and where his beard had been, there lingered yet a few grey tufts which seemed, like the ragged eyebrows, to denote the badness of the soil from which they sprung. The whole air and attitude of the form, was one of stealthy cat-like obsequiousness; the whole expression of the face was concentrated in a wrinkled leer, compounded of cunning, lecherousness, slyness, and avarice. (Chap. 47, p. 610)

By the time of *David Copperfield* and beyond, Pantaloon is still not entirely distinguishable from the villain—Mr. Spenlow, for instance, is comically compared to Punch and to the pantomime ogre, the Dragon of Wantley—but Clown is by this time entirely dissociated from Pantaloon, and the allegiance he must break is either to the wicked lover or to the evil principles or institutions he represents, which are usually the evils the novel itself opposes. Thus in *Bleak House* Guppy must overcome his awe of Tulkinghorn; in *A Tale of Two Cities* Sydney Carton must reject the selfish values of Lawyer Stryver, the lion to whom he has been playing jackal; and in *David Copperfield* Micawber must free himself from his bondage to Uriah Heep, for it is to this self-assertive social climber rather than to Mr. Wickfield, the Pantaloon, that Micawber has temporarily rented his soul.

Although the parents in *David Copperfield* do not symbolize the novel's evil as poignantly as the wicked lovers do, they always, at least, begin the trouble. This situation occurs in all Dickens' novels. Arthur A. Adrian, who has written the most comprehensive book about parent-child relationships in Dickens, deals in successive chapters with parents who are neglectful, destructive, wrong-headed, exploitive.[11] From John Willet of *Barnaby Rudge* to M.R.F. of *Our Mutual Friend*, they

---

11. Arthur A. Adrian, *Dickens and the Parent-Child Relationship* (Athens, Ohio: Ohio University Press, 1984).

prevent the heroes from living lives of their own. In *Women in the English Novel, 1800–1900,* Merryn Williams writes that the typical Dickensian heroine "from Madeline in *Nicholas Nickleby* to Lizzie in *Our Mutual Friend*" has a father "whom she unquestionably loves and supports although he usually does not deserve it."[12]

David Copperfield is an ideal work in which to investigate faulty parents because it contains such a variety of them. David and Steerforth each suffer from the absence of a judicious father, and Steerforth's live mother, like Uriah Heep's dead father, has taught him the lessons that eventually insure his undoing. Murdstone is in actuality rather than in fantasy the archetypal, usurping bad father of the Freudian family romance, as Clara is the typical weak and self-indulgent mother of the oedipal configuration. The presence of Micawber's children indicates his fecundity but also his irresponsibility, for he does not provide for them. In the Tommy Traddles plot Sophy is exploited by her parents, and Traddles is himself disinherited by his guardian simply because "he didn't like me when I grew up" (p. 345). Mr. Creakle has turned his son "out of doors" (p. 74). Indeed the only unequivocably good father in the novel seems to be the undertaker, Mr. Omer, who is also—and I believe this point to be of the highest significance—one of the few characters in the novel who can come to terms with the idea of death. He is also the most appreciative reader of David Copperfield's first novel.[13]

But the faulty parents on whom I wish to concentrate are the fathers, mothers, and guardians of the novel's four major heroines. These parents—Mr. Spenlow, Mrs. Markleham,

---

12. Merryn Williams, *Women in the English Novel, 1800–1900* (New York: St. Martin's Press, 1984), p. 75.
13. Mr. Omer tells the young writer, "What a lovely work that was of yours! What expressions in it! I read it every word—every word. And as to feeling sleepy! Not at all!" (p. 627). Before the interview ends, the old and dying man gives David his thoughts on mortality. "We are all drawing to the bottom of the hill, whatever age we are, on account of time never standing still for a single moment. So let us always do a kindness, and be overrejoiced. To be sure!" (p. 628).

Mr. Wickfield, and Mr. Peggotty—demonstrate various ways a parent can go wrong. Mrs. Markleham is perhaps selfish, and Spenlow is clearly self-absorbed, but none of these characters can be called evil. Wickfield loves his daughter deeply, and Mr. Daniel Peggotty is a model of parental benevolence. Nevertheless each of them is responsible not only for the troubles of the heroine he or she parents but also for letting loose the powers of evil that threaten her and the entire novel's stability. Pantaloon is not the villain, but he always plays directly into the villain's hand.[14]

Dora is little more than a phantom Columbine, and the constellation of male pantomime characters that surrounds her is both incomplete and something of a parody of the device that, as I am arguing, structures most of Dickens' plots and subplots. Julia Mills, Dora's comic Benevolent Spirit or Fairy Godmother, leaves the country, and there is no Clown in her story. The absence of these rescuing characters may be one reason for Dora's early death. No wicked lover threatens Dora's chastity unless it is David's rival at the picnic, the ominously named Red Whisker, whose beard color suggests perhaps a mild parody of the redheaded animal Uriah Heep. If David is her Harlequin, then he is not only ineffectual, which is not at all unusual for a Dickensian hero, but he is also disloyal and, so to speak, wishes her dead. Everything about this Little Blossom is faintly, sentimentally, even whimsically sketched, and so is her "little light-haired gentleman" of a father (p. 299). The touch is so delicate that I almost hesitate to burden Spenlow with the significance that, as I have said, belongs to Pantaloon in the Dickens pantomime.

Yet despite his brief and generally comical appearance in the action, Spenlow combines characteristics that illuminate a major theme of *David Copperfield* and that relate him meaningfully to the parents of the other heroines. To start with,

---

14. A good example is Gradgrind of *Hard Times,* whose Utilitarian philosophy is not precisely evil nor intended to harm but is so similar to James Harthouse's diabolism, as Dickens writes in his Number Plan, that Louisa is very nearly seduced.

Spenlow's profession unites two of the principal motifs of the novel, death and gentility. He is a proctor, which is a sort of probate attorney, and he also has to do professionally with wedding licenses and maritime law. Considering that *David Copperfield* is a study of marriages and of deaths, especially of deaths by drowning, we must wonder at all the critics who have dismissed the pages on Doctor's Commons as gratuitous satire, and we should admire Dickens all the more, who was able to embody an institution symbolic of so many of the concerns of his novel. In doing so, he was discovering, as we have heard Grahame Smith say, a new aspect of the novelist's craft,[15] and although he missed opportunities in *David Copperfield* that he would begin to make more of in *Bleak House*, Doctor's Commons was the apprentice step in the direction of Chancery, the Circumlocution Office, and the dust heaps.

A will can be seen as an attempt to defeat death, so to speak, by exercising power from the grave, or it can be the means of facing death and maturely arranging for the orderly transfer of worldly goods. In Spenlow's case the fear of death theme, which has predominated in *David Copperfield* from the second paragraph of the novel when the phantom-watching David hastens to assure us that he is not privileged to see ghosts, is expressed not only in Spenlow's occupation but also in his actions. For when he dies, it is discovered that he has been so unable to face the thought of death, that he has made no will for himself. He intentionally misinforms David on this point, claiming not only that his "testamentary arrangements," as he prefers to call his will, are completed and these "grave affairs long since composed," but also that the effect of having made "suitable provision" has been psychically satisfying. As David observes:

> There was a serenity, a tranquility, a calm-sunset air about him, which quite affected me. He was so peaceful and resigned—clearly had his affairs in such perfect train, and so systematically wound up—that he was a man to feel touched in the con-

---

15. See chap. 2, p. 34.

templation of. I really think I saw tears rise to his eyes, from the depth of his own feeling of all this. (Pp. 471–472)

But as Spenlow's clerk says when no will can be found, "If you had been in the Commons as long as I have, you would know that there is no subject on which men are so inconsistent, and so little to be trusted" (p. 476).

By permitting this probate attorney to die intestate, Dickens, I believe, is not simply indulging in a bit of pleasant irony. Spenlow was drawn to Doctor's Commons, as David was, and as the death-fearing Emily was drawn to work for an undertaker, precisely because of this obsession with dying. As we shall see, David and Emily both try to overcome death by giving themselves to Steerforth, who seems to represent and to offer a kind of aristocratic immortality. Gentility, as Dickens himself seemed to believe, at least near the beginning of his career, is what saves from death. It is the reason Oliver Twist and Rose Maylie live, while Little Dick and Nancy die. And gentility, according to both Steerforth and Spenlow, is what Doctor's Commons is principally about. "They plume themselves on their gentility there," Steerforth says, actually combining death and gentility in a single brilliant metaphor (p. 293). Spenlow's appearance as a genteel puppet-figure of death proves the validity of Steerforth's observation:

> He was buttoned up, mighty trim and tight, and must have taken a great deal of pains with his whiskers, which were accurately curled. His gold watch-chain was so massive, that a fancy came across me that he ought to have a sinewy golden arm, to draw it out with. . . . He was got up with such care, and was so stiff, that he could hardly bend himself. (P. 299)

When Spenlow gives David some hints in reference to their profession:

> He said it was the genteelest profession in the world, and must on no account be confounded with the profession of a solicitor: being quite another sort of thing, infinitely more exclusive, less mechanical, and more profitable. We took things much more easily in the Commons than could be taken anywhere else, he observed, and that set us, as a privileged class,

apart. He said it was impossible to conceal the disagreeable fact that we were chiefly employed by solicitors; but he gave me to understand that they were an inferior race of men, universally looked down upon by all proctors of any pretensions. (P. 331)

One reason Spenlow dies so ill-prepared, with "his affairs . . . in a most disordered state," is that "in the competition on all points of appearance and gentility then running high in the Commons, he had spent more than his professional income, which was not a very large one, and had reduced his private means, if they ever had been great (which was exceedingly doubtful) to a very low ebb indeed" (p. 477).

The influence of such a father on Dora's upbringing has been devastating. In *The Time Machine* H. G. Wells suggested that decorative helplessness would be the evolutionary effect of the concept of gentility, but Dickens earlier demonstrated this same process by describing it in just one generation. Sequestered in the Norwood villa and taught to take things with genteel ease, Dora is incapable of anything except attracting and charming someone like David, who is like her father in believing that gentility protects against death. Dora is subject to the same delusion, although in her case Dickens makes the point comically: "And Jip must have a mutton-chop every day at twelve," she insists, "or he'll die!" (p. 461). Like Bill Sikes' mongrel, Jip does die, this spoiled and genteel lapdog, simultaneously with his human double.[16] By then, however, Dora has overcome the fear of death that her father could not master, and she has provided a model of maturity for her still groping widower to emulate.

Mrs. Markleham is the sort of bad parent readers of *David Copperfield* would have been expecting from Dickens, the self-

---

16. The association between dog and mistress and the aristocratic pretensions of both are ironically supported by the dog's name and the place where David first encounters them. Norwood was the traditional home of the Gypsies, and Dora's dog was named Gyp in the manuscript. As if to emphasize

indulgent, exploitive parent who sells the child, usually in marriage, to secure his or her own comfort and security. The grossest example of the type occurs along with one of the first meaningful pantomime constellations, in *Nicholas Nickleby*, where the sybaritic Walter Bray allows himself to be persuaded that his daughter ought to be sacrificed to a salivating, old, lecherous miser so that he, Bray, may obtain "a new lease of life" (chap. 47, p. 621) and enjoy grapes and a newspaper. In the same novel Mrs. Nickleby shuts her eyes to the sexual exploitation of her daughter so that she may dream of an aristocratic connection. That Mrs. Nickleby was based on Dickens' own mother helps explain the anger that Dickens, himself an exploited child, felt toward this sort of bad parent. The character type appears in subsequent novels: In *Barnaby Rudge* John Chester urbanely tells his son that he has an obligation to marry for money because "I must have these little refinements about me. I have always been used to them, and I cannot exist without them" (chap. 15, p. 120); in *Martin Chuzzlewit* Pecksniff uses his daughter, no matter to him which daughter, to form the association with Jonas; and in *Dombey and Son* Mrs. Skewton in parallel with her relative, Good Mrs. Brown, urges her handsome daughter into prostitution and arranges the horse sale of Edith Granger. Mrs. Markleham is a somewhat tired example of a parent who sells a child, actually the last of the type to appear in Dickens,[17] although his best word on the irresponsible and exploitive parent would not be spoken until *Little Dorrit*. Mrs. Markleham does not compete at the level of either Mrs. Skewton or Mr. Dorrit, but she is, nevertheless, well worth considering.

---

the point, Dickens has David and Spenlow discuss Kotzebue's *The Stranger* on their way down to Norwood, where David will meet Dora. In the English translation of this play, with which Dickens was familiar, the Gypsy Queen comes from Norwood to speak the prologue, written by M. G. Lewis.

17. Gradgrind does not encourage Louisa to marry Bounderby for his own advantage; he is acting consistently with his philosophy. Subsequent parents try to dictate the marriage choices of their offspring, but never again, I think, with a purely commercial motive.

Hablot Browne, "Mr. Chester Takes His Ease," 1841, from *Barnaby Rudge*. Courtesy of the University of California at Riverside Library.

The Old Soldier differs from the other entrepreneurial parents in that she manages for her family rather than merely for herself and also in that the marriage she encourages turns out ironically to be a good one for her daughter, or at least Dickens would have us think so. Annie loved Doctor Strong purely and unreservedly from the start: "I never thought . . . of any worldly gain that my husband would bring me" (p. 563). We have seen that she did not even contemplate an infidelity with her cousin. Doctor Strong himself has never been willing to entertain even a suspicion regarding his wife's honor, and, unlike John Peerybingle of *The Cricket on the Hearth*, he has never been disposed to consider even briefly the possibility of violence toward the accused lover. The Strongs have been unhappy only on one another's behalf. The Doctor was saddened by the unfounded belief that he had hastened Annie into a marriage she now regrets, and Annie by the reflection that she has forced her husband to participate in her own "unmerited disgrace," the result of "the mean suspicion that my tenderness was bought—and sold to you, of all men, on earth" (p. 564). An older Dickens might have allowed this climate of suspicion to undermine the confidence of the Strongs in each other and, what might have been even more interesting, their confidence in themselves. Like Bella Wilfer of *Our Mutual Friend*, Annie Strong might have been brought to condemn herself as mercenary. Annie is a more self-respecting character, but she does not underestimate the unhappiness she has been made to feel or the potential harm of the estrangement she acts to end. Nor does she hesitate, unvindictively, to fix the blame on her faulty parent. "Mama, forgive me when I say that it was *you* who first presented to my mind the thought that anyone could wrong me, and wrong him, by such a suspicion" (p. 563).

Moreover, even if the Strongs were not in danger of losing confidence in themselves and in one another, the rest of the novel's world, as we have seen, was on shaky ground because of the uncertainty Mrs. Markleham initiated. The suspicion not only undermined David's essential confidence in the chastity of pure women, even including Agnes, it also increased the power of Uriah Heep, who used Annie's alleged infidelity as a card in his game to win Agnes. This was a practical gain for the opportunistic Heep, but it is not too much to say that the distrust of Annie Strong, which her mother initiates largely because she distrusts human nature and cannot credit the disinterested love of a young woman for an older man, increases Heep's power on a metaphysical level. The suspicion expands the power of evil in the novel and gives us our pantomimic Dark Scene, which, as we have noted, usually occurs, as it does here, in the melodramatic fifteenth number of a Dickens novel. The villain seems now to be in control; his view of the world and of human nature appears to have triumphed. In the pantomime the pursuers seize the magic wand that Harlequin has foolishly laid aside, and they flourish it over the terrified lovers. In Dickens, however, as in the pantomime, the Benevolent Agent is never far away, and at this moment in *David Copperfield* Aunt Betsey is present to call Mrs. Markleham a "marplot" (p. 562) and to pronounce that "there never would have been anything the matter, if it hadn't been for that old Animal" (p. 567).

We have already seen that the other character whose distrust has served as an accusation to Annie Strong is Mr. Wickfield, whose skepticism was indeed the germ of the novel, and who first entered Dickens' mind in association with his quintessential Pantaloon, Pecksniff. "What should you think of this for a notion of a character?" Dickens asked Forster in a letter of 19 January 1849. "'Yes, that is very true: but now, *What's his motive?*' I fancy I could make something like it into a kind of amusing and more innocent Pecksniff."[18] Obviously Dickens abandoned the idea of making Wickfield's skepticism amusing—he had, in fact, done better in this regard with Mr. Grimwig of *Oliver Twist*—and he must also have thought again

18. Letter to Forster, 19 January 1849, quoted in *The Life of Charles Dickens*, p. 524.

about Wickfield's innocence, for although there is no self-interest in his habitual distrust of human nature, the Hobbesian premises on which Wickfield operates, especially the assumption that everyone, himself included, is essentially motivated by self-interest, are the reverse of innocence. Indeed Wickfield's is the mean and sophisticated worldview that the novel *David Copperfield* must overcome before its narrator and central character can achieve a disciplined heart, without alloy of self, and become the hero of his own life.

Wickfield is not an exploitive parent like Mrs. Markleham, but he has at least one predecessor among the bad parents of the earlier novels. Like Nell's Grandfather in *The Old Curiosity Shop*, he loves the child so well that he renders himself helpless and burdens her with the responsibility of acting the part of parent to him. Old Trent becomes an obsessive gambler for Nell's sake; Wickfield, prefiguring Mr. Dolls of *Our Mutual Friend*, is an alcoholic. Agnes, like the typical child of an addict, sacrifices her youth in order to do for him, and she also feels guilty for his condition:

> "I almost feel as if I had been papa's enemy, instead of his loving child. For I know how he has altered, in his devotion to me. I know how he has narrowed the circle of his sympathies and duties, in the concentration of his whole mind upon me. I know what a multitude of things he has shut out for my sake, and how his anxious thoughts of me have shadowed his life, and weakened his strength and energy, by turning them always upon one idea. If I could ever set this right! If I could ever work out his restoration, as I have so innocently been the cause of his decline." (P. 316)

Wickfield's relationship with Agnes is not a simple reversal of the father-daughter relationship, for he loves Agnes in place of his dead wife, whose portrait she resembles and whose domestic duties she has been encouraged to assume. Theirs is one of the several January-May relationships in *David Copperfield*, which have caused at least one critic to conclude that Dickens (at age thirty-seven!) was betrayed into "a widespread pattern of uncertainty and confusion . . . by an unconscious predilection for the attachment between elderly men and youthful women."[19] A distinction needs to be made, however, between relationships where the husband is taking the place of the wife's dead father, as, for instance, in the Strong marriage and in Clara Copperfield's first marriage, and in marriagelike relationships where the child is forced to substitute for the dead spouse. Dickens seems to approve when Annie Strong values the doctor as her father and her husband, but he is as uneasy as the reader is at the sickly sexual relationship of the Heeps, mother and child, and of Mrs. Steerforth's feelings for her son, "who has been the object of my life, to whom every thought has been devoted, whom I have gratified from a child in every wish, from whom I have had no separate existence since his birth" (p. 401). There can be no doubt of Dickens' disapproval of the relationship between Agnes and her father, which Wickfield himself comes to call "sordid" (p. 494) and "diseased" (p. 721). "My natural grief for my child's mother turned to disease; my natural love for my child turned to disease. I have infected everything I touched" (p. 493). Sylvia Manning has written that Wickfield's neurotic attachment to Agnes is the cause of his own near destruction and that such daughter/father pairings in Dickens "tend to keep the woman a child . . . [because] the inversion creates a single daughter-wife-mother figure, and . . . that wife-mother is a little girl."[20] In the case of Agnes it has also deprived her of her childhood. Meisel goes much farther, pointing out that "the underside of the transfigured image of the saving daughter . . . [is] the horror of the scene in Ugolino's tower," in which Dante presents the child offering himself as food to the starving parent.[21]

---

19. Brian Crick, " 'Mr Peggotty's Dream Comes True': Fathers and Husbands; Wives and Daughters," *University of Toronto Quarterly* 54 (1984): 40.
20. Sylvia Manning, "Dickens, January, May," *The Dickensian* 71 (1975): 71.
21. *Realizations*, p. 306. Meisel is writing with particular reference to the relationship between Amy Dorrit and her father. Another critic of that same novel, Peter Smith, comments on the "cloying quasi-sexual nastiness in the bond between" Pet Meagles and her father. Peter Smith, *Public and Private Value: Studies in the Nineteenth-Century Novel* (Cambridge: Cambridge University Press, 1984), p. 20.

Since Agnes is the exclusive motive of his own life, Wickfield has concluded that everyone acts on one clear—and selfish—motive. Thinking that he "could truly love one creature in the world, and not love the rest . . . truly mourn for one creature gone out of the world, and not have some part in the grief of all that mourned" (p. 493), he has closed off his human sympathies. He is thus another example in the novel of the destructive power of the fear of death. And, of course, he and his skeptical philosophy are more directly responsible than even Mrs. Markleham and her cynicism for letting loose the evil of Uriah Heep, for Heep is the Genie that Wickfield has let out of the bottle. "I looked for single motives in every one," he tells David when he recognizes at last just what Heep wants to accomplish and how much power he has irresponsibly been given. "I was satisfied I had bound him to me by motives of interest. But see what he is—oh, see what he is!" (p. 493). Wickfield thus shows how even a very loving father can play the part of the panto Pantaloon in setting afoot all the real and symbolic mischief of the plot.

Until Q. D. Leavis discovered similarities between Wickfield's love for Agnes and Daniel Peggotty's "horribly possessive love" for Emily, Mr. Peggotty, although a bachelor, used to be regarded as the best father in Dickens and perhaps in all of nineteenth-century literature. He has made his whimsical home into a haven for two orphans and a widow; he rejoices in his niece's forthcoming marriage, and when she falls, he more than forgives her; he dedicates his life to her reclamation. Surely Mrs. Leavis goes too far when she calls Mr. Peggotty's devotion "maniacal,"[22] but her insight cannot be gainsaid, and subsequent critics have taken it up, pointing out, for instance, that Mr. Peggotty is the active force in Ham's courtship of Emily, that Emily holds on to Mr. Peggotty, "clinging . . . to him, tighter and tighter, and closer and closer, every

22. Q. D. Leavis, "Dickens and Tolstoy," in *Dickens the Novelist*, by F. R. Leavis and Q. D. Leavis, p. 79.

day" (p. 376), and that when his "dream comes true" (p. 609), and he reclaims her from Steerforth at last, "all night long, her arms has been about my neck, and her head has laid heer; and we knows full well, as we can put our trust in one another, ever more" (p. 623). Brian Crick notes that when David and Steerforth interrupt the moment of Emily's engagement, she is "in the act of flying into Daniel Peggotty's arms, not those of her fiance," and Philip M. Weinstein points out that "the scene is so imagined by Dickens and conveyed to the reader that the voice of overriding affection belongs to Mr. Peggotty."[23] Both critics comment on the similarity to the diseased relationship of Mr. Wickfield and his daughter.

There is another interesting similarity between the two fathers. Just as Wickfield is afraid that contact with Annie Strong may corrupt Agnes, so Mr. Peggotty could not bear to see Emily in conversation with Martha Endell, the fallen woman who will ultimately save her. As Ham says, "He couldn't, kind-natur'd, tender-hearted as he is, see them two together, side by side, for all the treasures that's wrecked in the sea" (p. 287). Mr. Peggotty thus displays the same suspicion of human nature that Wickfield does. In this case the lack of faith may have played a part in the fall of the woman Mr. Peggotty sought to protect, for his distrustful attitude forces Emily to her first questionable action, her secret meeting with Martha.

Most surprising of all is the similarity between Daniel Peggotty and another of the faulty fathers we have discussed, Mr. Spenlow, a similarity in respect to the concept of gentility, of all things. Mr. Peggotty has been regarded not only as the quintessentially good father of Victorian fiction but also as the most self-respecting proletarian character in Dickens.[24] I do not wish to contradict either of these perceptions, but just as it is true that Mr. Peggotty's love for Emily is too

---

23. Crick, "'Mr. Peggotty's Dream Comes True'," pp. 51–52; Philip M. Weinstein, *The Semantics of Desire: Changing Models of Identity from Dickens to Joyce* (Princeton: Princeton University Press, 1984), p. 38.

24. See John Jordan, "The Social Sub-Text of *David Copperfield*," *Dickens Studies Annual* 14, ed. Michael Timko, Fred Kaplan, Edward Guiliano (New York: AMS Press, 1985), pp. 61–92.

complicated for simple definition, it must also be noted that he is seduced by Steerforth long before his niece Emily is.

As the novel was originally conceived, it was Clara Peggotty rather than her brother who was to visit David at Salem House and meet Steerforth. The change in plans allows us to see a side of this humble man of the sea that might otherwise be less apparent, his high regard for gentility. Pride is David's motive for making the introduction:

> I am not sure whether it was in the pride of having such a friend as Steerforth, or in the desire to explain to him how I came to have such a friend as Peggotty, that I called to him [Steerforth] as he was going away. (P. 89)

But if we fear a collision between these two seemingly opposite characters, or a humiliation for Mr. Peggotty of the sort Steerforth deals Mr. Mell, we are soon relieved. Steerforth promptly charms Mr. Peggotty, and Mr. Peggotty shows a ready disposition to *be* charmed. Before the scene is over, he has invited Steerforth to make the visit to Yarmouth that years later will produce such dire consequences. "My house ain't much to see, sir, but it's hearty at your service, if you should ever come along with Mas'r Davy to see it" (p. 90). (Note Mr. Peggotty's ways of referring to those he considers his betters.) A few pages later, he will talk Steerforth up at home with an enthusiasm that may well have initiated Emily's romantic infatuation about him: "'There's a friend!' said Mr. Peggotty, stretching out his pipe. 'There's a friend, if you talk of friends! Why, Lord love my heart alive, if it ain't a treat to look at him!'" (p. 122).

Emily's infatuation with gentility predates her own meeting with Steerforth. As Mr. Omer the undertaker points out, it has made her unpopular in Yarmouth: "An ill-natured story got about that Emily wanted to be a lady" (p. 260). As David and the reader both know, this ambition began even before Mr. Peggotty's meeting with Steerforth: She voiced it on the Yarmouth beach in the very first number of the novel when she reflected on the class differences between herself and David. This desire to rise in station may have come from Mr.

Peggotty, for he appears to have given her a necklace of blue beads (p. 27). An aspect of the description of his house not only suggests a possible pretention to gentility but also comments on it and foreshadows the perils of such an ambition:

> On the chest of drawers there was a tea-tray with a painting on it of a lady with a parasol, taking a walk with a military-looking child who was trundling a hoop. The tray was kept from tumbling down, by a bible; and the tray [the bible in MS A] if it had tumbled down, would have smashed a quantity of cups and saucers that were grouped around the book. (P. 26)

But whether or not Emily got the idea from her uncle, it is anyways certain that she wants to become a lady for his sake. Mr. Omer thinks that the story of Emily's wanting to be a lady "came into circulation principally on account of her sometimes saying, at the school, that if she was a lady she would like to do so and so for her uncle—don't you see—and buy him such and such fine things" (p. 260). And, indeed, on the Yarmouth beach she told David, "If I was ever to be a lady, I'd give him a sky-blue coat with diamond buttons, nankeen trousers, a red velvet waistcoat, a cocked hat, a large gold watch, a silver pipe, and a box of money" (p. 30).[25] But it is not only the trappings of gentility Emily desires for her uncle. Her next speech connects her ambition, and perhaps her uncle's as well, to the fear of death, which, as we saw in our treatment of Spenlow, is related in *David Copperfield* to the ambitious dream of gentility.

> We could all be gentlefolk together, then. Me and uncle, and Ham, and Mrs. Gummidge. We wouldn't mind then, when there come stormy weather.—Not for our own sakes, I mean. We would for the poor fishermen's, to be sure, and we'd help 'em with money when they came to any hurt. . . . I wake when it blows, and I tremble to think of uncle Dan and Ham,

---

25. As Scott Moncrieff has pointed out in his dissertation, "Dickens and the Reformulated Family" (University of California at Riverside, 1988), p. 198, the gentlemanly blue jacket and the nankeen trousers that Emily intends to give to her uncle end up on Mr. Wickfield when we first see him.

and believe I hear 'em crying out for help. That's why I should
like so much to be a lady. (Pp. 30–31)

This speech provides the essential link between the apparently disparate themes in *David Copperfield* of gentility and the fear of death. In the mind of a vulnerable little girl who has seen her own father and most of the fathers around her "drowndead," gentility means at its most basic level that one need not take the boat out in dangerous weather. It is, of course, one of the supreme ironies of the novel that the gentleman she hopes will confer this genteel immortality should himself drown in a pleasure craft, but the mistake is so rational, so understandable as to make Emily's motive for wanting to become a lady believable not only for her but for everyone in the novel, including her bluff uncle, who, as we have seen, asks the *Lord* to love his heart *alive* (p. 122; emphases added).

The four parents I have considered are all well-meaning, and yet, like Pantaloon, they all do damage to set the plots afoot. Daniel Peggotty, who is the best of them, does the most harm, and serves better than any of them to connect the themes of distrust of human nature and ambition for gentility with the fear of death, which overshadows the posthumous and ghost-haunted novel he figures in. As representatives of a hierarchy that had elevated the concept of gentility in the nineteenth century to a status equivalent to the chivalric codes of earlier times, these parents, no matter how loving and well-meaning, needed to be, as Dickens well knew, both discredited and overthrown.

5

Dandy Lover: Death and the Gentleman

> "Very well," said Mrs. Quilp, nodding her head, "as I said just now, it's very easy to talk, but I say again that I know—that I'm sure—Quilp has such a way with him when he likes, that the best-looking woman here couldn't refuse him if I was dead, and she free, and he chose to make love to her."
>
> —*The Old Curiosity Shop*

Lover had virtually disappeared from the pantomime by the middle 1830s. Planché remembered this character strongly, perhaps because his own early pantomime, *Rodolph the Wolf; or, Columbine Red Riding-Hood* (1818), gave Lover the principal role. Although this villainous and/or foppish suitor of Columbine can be found as early as *Harlequin's Chaplet* (1790), his was an optional part even in the Regency pantomime, where sometimes he appeared only in the opening or was transformed to Clown or even Pantaloon when the comic business began. Dandy Lover is nevertheless an essential part of Dickens' vision and of his pantomime.

David Mayer demonstrates some ways in which this character was used to satirize dandies and "dandy manners" of the Regency.[1] Dickens, whose own waistcoats were considered somewhat extravagant, was not interested in ridiculing dandyism except when he could expose it as Carlylean dilettantism in a Turveydrop or a Gowan, and although Arthur Gride may be inordinately proud of his bottle-green suit and

---

1. David Mayer, "Dandyism in Regency Pantomime," *Theatre Notebook*, 19 (1965): 96.

Dandy Lover, from a Juvenile Drama Sheet, circa 1830.

Carker the Manager cuts an elegantly catlike figure, foppish dress and behavior are not usually important features of Dickens' unsuitable lovers. Nevertheless the character in Dickens' fiction closely related to the Dandy Lover in pantomime is usually the one who most clearly expresses the negative side of the author's social vision.

Dandy Lover is also the pantomime character with the strongest connections to melodrama. He is, in many respects, a trivialized version of the melodramatic villain, who remained throughout the nineteenth century the best dressed, or at least the most overdressed, character on the stage. Since melodrama was a child of the French Revolution, it frequently vented its anger at the oppressive power of an illegitimate hierarchy, and the villain's evening dress thus became a symbol of class.

Dickens, as we have seen, tended sometimes to conflate similar figures from pantomime and melodrama. More frequently he used a character taken from one genre to parody a figure derived from the other. Thus in *Nicholas Nickleby* the cowardly and ridiculous Arthur Gride stands as a comment on the arrogantly powerful Sir Mulberry Hawk. Both characters play similar roles in their separate plots: Each poses the chief sexual threat to the heroine; each has power over the girl's father or guardian; and each appears to have direct or indirect control over the character I am identifying as the Clown, in the case of *Nicholas Nickleby*, Newman Noggs and Lord Frederick Verisopht, respectively.

For all his timid foolishness, Gride seems to be the more significant of the two villains. He operates in the mercenary plot of the novel and represents "the world," which his partner, Ralph Nickleby, claims with confident authority to "know" (chap. 44, p. 575). Gride and Ralph Nickleby thus seem to embody the principal wickedness in Dickens' vision in 1838–39, commercial worldliness, whereas Sir Mulberry has been dismissed by critics as a stock villain, merely a wicked aristocrat. The distinction is essentially correct in terms of Dickens' conscious intentions, but it ignores the theme of gentility, destined, as we have just seen, to become a major concern of Dickens' maturity, a theme that finds its first tentative expression in this early novel. As the orphaned son of an impoverished gentleman, Nicholas is as desperate to establish his gentlemanly status as David Copperfield or Pip is.[2] He is as snobbishly condescending to the Kenwigses and the Crummles, whom he does not even trust with his real name, as Pip is to Joe Gargery or David is to the Peggottys. Unlike James Steerforth, Sir Mulberry is hardly a model for the would-be gentleman-hero, but, like Bentley Drummle of *Great Expectations,* he is a "glaring instance," indicating (to the reader at least) the shallowness of the hero's dream of gentility. Although Dickens' social theme changes from novel to novel, this essential relationship between hero (or Harlequin) and villain (or Dandy Lover) recurs frequently in the early novels. Young Martin Chuzzlewit becomes Pecksniff's student, not simply so he can learn architecture, but because they are kindred in spirit as in blood. Walter Gay is sent to Dombey and Son's to be made into another James Carker, a successful manager, a self-made man on the model, so Walter's naive friends would believe, of the legendary Dick Whittington. In this case, interestingly, it is the catlike Carker who sends the ambitious merchant's apprentice on a voyage to be sold.

It is clearer in *David Copperfield* than in *Nicholas Nickleby* (although not nearly as clear as it was later to become in *Great Expectations*) that Dickens was fully aware of the unworthiness of his hero's aspiration to gentility. David's great difficulty with servants, who seem always to be taking advantage of him or finding him out, is a constant, comical reminder of

2. When Nicholas accepts his uncle's proposition about teaching at Dotheboys Hall, he is "delighted with a thousand visionary ideas," especially one about becoming the friend and traveling companion of some "young nobleman who is being educated at the Hall" and who later procures "a handsome appointment for him and marries Kate" (chap. 3, p. 27). Ralph Nickleby, who shrewdly sizes his nephew up from this speech, assumes falsely that Nicholas's attachment to Smike is motivated by the "romance" that he is a "persecuted descendant of a man of high degree" and takes pleasure in smashing the genteel illusion. "You shall see," he tells Nicholas, "how your sympathy melts before plain matter of fact" (chap. 45, p. 594).

the class uncertainty of this governess's son. Still there are so many competing issues in *David Copperfield*—the examination of marriage, the obsession with death, the problem of the undisciplined heart, and so on—that the Dandy Lovers of the novel are perhaps necessary to keep a sharp focus on the work's social theme.

In her study of the Dandy, Ellen Moers sees James Steerforth as an important transitional figure for Dickens, who, "for the first time draws a character whose 'aristocratic' temperament, manners and attitudes play a major part in the novel. Steerforth the wicked seducer is merely a repetition of immature melodrama; but Steerforth, the schoolboy hero of David Copperfield, is Dickens' first attempt to deal with a problem that would bedevil him in maturity.[3] But although the distinction that Moers makes between Steerforth the seducer of Emily and Steerforth the seducer of David can lead to interesting speculation about Dickens' and David's feelings of gender ambivalence, it need not imply a difference of social vision.

In his public reading of *David Copperfield* Dickens introduced Steerforth by adding these words to the text: "Steerforth, half a dozen years older than I; brilliant, handsome, easy, winning; whom I admired with my whole heart; for whom I entertained the most romantic feelings of fidelity and friendship."[4] Obviously these are the genteel qualities that attracted Emily as well, but in both cases Steerforth's aristocratic manners were seductive not only for their own sakes but also for the mastery they seemed to represent and confer. "He was a person of great power in my eyes," writes David (p. 76), who recalls being "carried" before Steerforth at their first meeting, "as before a magistrate" (p. 72). What Steerforth's power seems to confer upon David on this occasion is no less a boon than the human identity that Murdstone, with

---

3. Ellen Moers, *The Dandy: Brummell to Beerbohm* (New York: Viking Press, 1960), pp. 229–30.
4. *Charles Dickens: The Public Readings*, ed. Philip Collins (Oxford: The Clarendon Press, 1975), p. 220.

his beatings and his dog sign, had taken away from him. Like Minos, judge of the underworld, Steerforth "enquired, under a shed in the playground, into the particulars of my punishment, and was pleased to express his opinion that it was 'a jolly shame,' for which I became bound to him ever afterwards" (p. 72). Murdstone, the dark gentleman, whom the critic Barry Westburg correctly identifies as "the resurrection of death itself, of life's primal antithesis," has been defeated, it would appear, by this new gentleman, "the incarnated dream of invincible vitality," as Garrett Stewart calls him, and "under a shed," no less.[5] In a novel about a posthumous child who finds himself surrounded by death on all sides and who is subject to nightmare fears of the graveyard, the power the gentlemanly Steerforth seems to offer is highly attractive, as it is also to Emily, who has a "dread of death" (p. 379) and who has lost so many "drowndead" friends and relatives. In Emily's case the protection that gentility appears to promise is much more than simply metaphorical. As we have seen, the destructive ambition to become a lady had its roots in her practical observation that gentlefolk did not need to risk their lives on the stormy ocean. Thus when Steerforth appears in her life and offers to take Emily away from her work at the undertakers', it is not just a matter of innocent maiden and melodramatic seducer, at least not unless we are ready to afford Dickensian melodrama and the Dickens pantomime a most serious reading.

Such a reading goes on to note that, of course, neither Dandy Lover nor his counterpart in the melodrama ever intends to keep the promise of immortality he appears to make or that he could keep it if he wished. Steerforth, as his treatment of Mr. Mell and Ham Peggotty and as his attitudes toward the poor in general amply testify, has no sympathies for those whom he regards as beneath him. He thinks that they

---

5. Barry Westburg, *The Confessional Fictions of Charles Dickens* (DeKalb: Northern Illinois University Press, 1977), p. 46; Garrett Stewart, *Death Sentences: Styles of Dying in British Fiction* (Cambridge, Mass.: Harvard University Press, 1984), p. 78.

belong to a different species and that they do not feel pain as gentlefolk do. Moreover, as the story itself proves, he is himself very far from waterproof. Indeed Steerforth is subject to the same delusion that had misled David and Emily and, as Dickens understood it, the entire Victorian society: the mistaken notion that gentility saves. Arnold Kettle has written that the idealization of Steerforth, "the Byronic superman, aristocratic self-confidence and all, is revealed in the novel as no arbitrary personal 'weakness' in David's character, but as a complex, socio/psychological problem of nineteenth-century England."[6] Tennyson saw the gentleman as the aim of evolutionary change, and Newman thought it was the chief business of the university to produce him. Characters in Dickens—Pip, for instance, who finds himself mired in the marshes—aspire to gentility as to the stars, where an existence free of pain, suffering, shame, humiliation, and even death seems somehow possible. Steerforth, who rides "rough-shod, if need be, smooth-shod, if that will do" (p. 364) in a race he cannot name, loses it at last on the same Yarmouth beach where Emily dreamed of saving herself and her family by becoming a lady.

Steerforth never achieves a clear understanding of his actions, nor do those around him. He regards his own "gentlemanly" behavior as "fitfulness" (p. 276). David concludes that Steerforth was playing "a brilliant game . . . for the excitement of the moment, for the employment of high spirits, in the thoughtless love of superiority, in a mere wasteful careless course of winning what was worthless to him, and next minute thrown away" (p. 265). Rosa Dartle, who also loves him, only wants to know what is leading him: "Is it anger, is it hatred, is it pride, is it restlessness, is it some wild fancy, is it love, *what is it?*" (p. 369). What, indeed?

Steerforth's mother, perhaps the greatest influence in forming her son's character, proudly explains his behavior at

---

6. Arnold Kettle, "Thoughts on 'David Copperfield'," *Review of English Literature* 2 (July 1961): 73.

school: "He would have risen against all constraint; but he found himself the monarch of the place, and he haughtily determined to be worthy of his station. It was like himself" (p. 253). We are never given explicitly to understand the motives behind Mrs. Steerforth's desire to form an aristocratic temperament in her son, nor are we ever told why she takes such satisfaction in the results, but her word *risen* may provide a clue. Like so many other widowed parents in the novel—Mr. Wickfield, Mrs. Heep, Clara Copperfield—Mrs. Steerforth lives in a kind of romantic relationship with her son and has more invested in him than a mother ought. Scarred once by death, these parents are perhaps seeking to outwit it in their children. In the case of Mrs. Steerforth, power, aristocratic power, may appear to be the best way of rising "against all constraint." When her son declasses himself by running off with Emily, he becomes dead to her, and she becomes a sort of ghost.

Immediately after his reunion with Steerforth in London and following the performance of *Julius Caesar*, David dreams of the immortal gods. Steerforth has just rescued David from a small gravelike bedchamber at the inn, a room "shut up like a family vault" (p. 243). Emily seems to expect something like a rebirth from Steerforth, hoping for the day "he *brings me back* a lady" (p. 386, emphasis added). Idolized by the desperate needs of all these death dreaders, Steerforth understandably mistakes his own nature and drives headlong to his own and to their destruction. It is a mark of Dickens' extraordinary sympathy for this essentially villainous character that he permits him to pause momentarily along the way and wish to God he "had had a steadfast and judicious father these last twenty years" (p. 275).

The Dandy Lover or melodramatic villain who believes he benefited most from the counsel of a judicious father is Steerforth's opposite in the novel, Uriah Heep, who has based the conduct of his entire life on his father's wise admonition to "Be umble" (p. 490). As a result of following this most Christian advice, Heep's father himself has risen on the social scale, if not in this world then in the next, where he is "a partaker of glory at present" (p. 200). Interestingly, the senior Heep's former, more humble, calling, like David's work at Spenlow and Jorkins' and Emily's at Omer and Joram's, was connected with death: He was a sexton.

The sexton's son, Uriah Heep, who is as sophisticated a development of Arthur Gride of *Nicholas Nickleby* as James Steerforth is of Sir Mulberry Hawk, is also trying, with an existential desperation, to dig himself out. Making use of a hypocritical show of Christian virtue and with a true commitment to the Protestant work ethic and the doctrine of selfhelp, Uriah Heep is seeking, against all constraint, to rise in *this* world. And it does not trivialize his genuine attraction for Agnes Wickfield any more than it diminishes David's passion for Dora Spenlow to observe that a great part of what Uriah sees in Agnes is her station as the daughter of a gentleman. In the terms of *David Copperfield* and in terms most Victorians would understand, rising in the world and gaining the love, or at least the person, of a pure and genteel woman are both the means and the signs of a young man's salvation.

Of course David sees no similarity between his ambition to marry *his* master's daughter and the impudence of "this detestable Rufus with the mulberry-colored great-coat" (p. 329) in regard to Agnes. David would be even more outraged, if possible, at any comparison between Heep and Steerforth, who are as far separated in his cosmology as Magwitch and Estella, father and daughter, are in Pip's. But in fact David loves the same women whom Heep and Steerforth love. And although he is repulsed by the one villain and charmed by the other, he is fascinated, perhaps equally, by both. As A.O.J. Cockshut writes of David's obsession with Uriah, "Physical repulsion, moral disapproval, and class superiority are mingled, are boiled up together into a kind of broth where they become indistinguishable."[7] Both Steerforth and Heep have

---

7. Cockshut, *The Imagination of Charles Dickens*, p. 119. David is puzzled sometimes by his reactions to Uriah. At one point he confesses to "feeling

frequently been seen as doubles of David, the one representing David as he would like to be, the other reflecting him as he fears he really is, and the language of the novel, David's language, contains as much special pleading in favor of the one character as it does unfair condemnation of the other.

The two doubles never meet in the action of the novel, but we surely know what Steerforth would think of Heep because, for one thing, we see him in relation to his ambitious servant Littimer. And Heep would doubtlessly react to Steerforth as he does to Jack Maldon, who plays Dandy Lover in the Annie Strong plot. "He never could come into the office, without ordering and shoving me about," Heep says of Maldon. "One of your fine gentlemen he was! I was very meek and umble—and I am. But I didn't like that sort of thing—and I don't!" (p. 519). In *Our Mutual Friend* where the Heep and Steerforth characters do come together and confront one another in the persons of Bradley Headstone and Eugene Wrayburn, the same attitudes produce an even greater antipathy, but the pre–Nietzschean *ressentiment* that Heep feels at the humiliations of the class system he is seeking to conquer had already found expression in *Dombey and Son*, where Carker the Manager burns with a hatred directed both at his own subservient position and at the master he imitates and pretends to admire. Thus Carker says of Mr. Dombey:

> There is not a man employed here [in the office of Dombey and Son] . . . who wouldn't be glad at heart to see his master humbled: who does not hate him, secretly: who does not wish him evil rather than good: and who would not turn upon him, if he had the power and boldness. The nearer to his favour, the nearer to his insolence. (Chap. 46, p. 616)

Heep plots against Wickfield in a similar spirit, which David calls "base, unrelenting, and revengeful" (p. 491). He strives

---

myself attracted towards Uriah Heep, who had a sort of fascination for me" (p. 200). Later, when Heep is sleeping in David's sitting room, David is "attracted to him in very repulsion, and could not help wandering in and out every half hour or so, and taking another look at him" (p. 328).

not only for his own advancement but also for his master's destruction. And it would not be enough for Heep merely to marry his Columbine, he must also pollute her.

Enough has been said to indicate how powerfully destructive a character the unsuitable lover is. His nature as tempter and wicked seducer is also understandable in terms of his literary origins in pantomime, melodrama, Gothic fiction, Byron, Richardson, and Restoration drama, and even in *Paradise Lost* and earlier works involving the devil.[8] What is surprising is only the fact we have been noting: In Dickens the unsuitable lover is not only the cause of evil; he is also one of the victims of it. Steerforth is as much deluded by the mad notion that gentility saves from death as are the more sympathetic characters, and he pays for his delusion more dramatically than most of the others. Similarly Heep is not only the oppressive villain of melodrama, he is also the victim of the very social system that revolutionary melodrama thought it was trying to overthrow. The resentful anger that Heep, Carker, and Headstone so clearly express is the emotion that usually generates melodramatic action and that the villain is supposed to inspire in the audience rather than feel himself. Is it any wonder that Dickens is confusing to revolutionaries and that they find him finally so unsatisfactory?

This is not by any means to say that readers do not become enraged at Steerforth and disgusted with Heep. Clearly they do, and Dickens seems strongly to encourage this outrage. Since we identify with the narrator, we resent Steerforth's continual air of condescension toward him, even though David seems to delight in it, and we share David's repulsion for Heep, whom Dickens appears sometimes to equate with one of the most hateful of his Dandy Lovers, Daniel Quilp. In a scene reminiscent of Nell's last moments before leaving the

---

8. Harry Stone has written, "Uriah is a species of devil. This is no metaphor, but a part of Uriah's menacing reality. His infernal origins are implicit in his cadaverous face, red hair, sleepless red eyes, skeleton hand, and snaky writhing." "Dickens and Fantasy: The Case of Uriah Heep," *The Dickensian* 75 (1979): 97. In a canceled passage of *David Copperfield* Uriah invokes "the Devil's name" (p. 644).

Old Curiosity Shop, for instance, David observes the sleeping Heep. Nell had seen Quilp "hanging so far out of [her] bed that he almost seemed to be standing on his head . . . gasping and growling with his mouth wide open, and the whites (or rather the dirty yellows) of his eyes distinctly visible" (chap. 12, p. 96). David describes Heep similarly, "lying on his back, with his legs extending to I don't know where, gurglings taking place in his throat, stoppages in his nose, and his mouth open like a post-office" (p. 328). Both passages are potentially comic, but the reader cannot help sharing the narrators' disgust. Nor can the reader help identifying with David when he is so upset at "the image of Agnes, outraged by so much as a thought of this red-headed animal," that he becomes obsessed with "a delirious idea of seizing the red-hot poker out of the fire, and running him through with it" (p. 326). Never mind that the red-hot poker bit was one of the most standard and hilarious of harlequinade routines.

But, of course, we do mind, if only subliminally. For all the surface similarity in plot and characters, the visions of melodrama and pantomime are essentially at odds with one another. Can Heep be both dangerous and ridiculous? Perhaps so. Think of Chaplin's Great Dictator. Can a villain be both a victim of circumstances and the object of comic outrage? Steerforth apparently can be both seducer and seduced. So confusing and subversive a vision, though, requires a more complex genre than melodrama, which, for all its power, is relatively humorless and simple-minded, depending, as we have heard Christopher Prendergast say, on the elementary rhetorical figures of "antithesis and hyperbole."[9] Pantomime, from which melodrama sprung in a historical moment of rage, provides the more comprehensive vision within which villains can be transformed by a wave of the fairy's wand into comical fellows, the victims of their own greed and awkwardness and of an absurd universe. Thus in the first transformation scene of Planché's *Rodolph the Wolf; or, Columbine*

---

9. See chap. 2, p. 34.

Hablot Browne, "Quilp's Grotesque Politeness," 1840, from *The Old Curiosity Shop.* Courtesy of the University of California at Riverside Library.

Red Riding-Hood the Benevolent Agent touches the wicked seducer with her wand and says:

> For thee whose heart ne'er bred but black intent
> To ruin nature's fairest ornament;
> Thus thy career of wickedness I stop:
> Be that most imbecile of things—a fop.[10]

And a world that seemed ready to be swallowed up in anger is redeemed suddenly by expiative comedy.

Dickens does not let his villains off the hook so easily. Usually he drowns them or shoots them or tears them to pieces under the wheels of railway engines, although he cannot resist sometimes, as in the cases of Pecksniff and Heep, allowing them to rise from humiliation at the last moment to make a grand show of forgiving their enemies. Their defeat, however, is never the melodramatic last word of the drama, which in Dickens, as in pantomime, is one of reconciliation. Dickens' Dandy Lovers compel our interest to the penultimate instant, but we end always with our good thoughts focused on the love of Harlequin and Columbine.

---

10. James Robinson Planché, *Rodolph the Wolf; or, Columbine Red Riding-Hood* (London: John Lowndes, 1819). Performed at the Olympic New Theatre, 21 December 1818.

6

Harlequin: The Guilty Hero

> At the end of the book you know Micawber, whereas you only know what happened to David, and are not interested enough in him to wonder what his politics or religion might be if anything so stupendous as a religious or political idea, or general idea of any sort, were to occur to him. He is tolerable as a child; but he never becomes a man, and he might as well be left out of his biography altogether but for his usefulness as a stage confidant, a Horatio or "Charles his friend": what they call on the stage a feeder.
> —George Bernard Shaw

> Harlequin is the worst part in a Pantomime—a thing of shreds and patches.
> —Tom Dibden

The anger that audiences of melodrama invariably directed at the villain is frequently aimed by readers of Dickens at the hero. This is a curious business. The hero in the melodrama is usually stupid, and it is easy enough to forget about the young lover of Gothic romance until, not before the final chapter, he rescues the girl, still technically a virgin but sadly deflowered psychologically by her hate affair with the more sexually energetic villain. But in neither of these forms are we quite tempted to hiss the hero, as we have just heard Shaw do in the case of David Copperfield.

David is simply one of many seemingly innocuous heroes in Dickens, and he does not by any means get the worst of it either from readers or from fellow characters. I suppose that distinction must be reserved for Charles Darnay, who is indicted by an English court, condemned by a French tribunal, and despised by nearly everyone inside and outside *A Tale of*

Two Cities, characters and readers alike. Darnay's aristocratic uncle wants him dead, and the peasant Madame Defarge has him prominently in her knitting. Lawyer Stryver asserts, "There is contamination in such a scoundrel" (bk. 2, chap. 24, p. 228), and even Sydney Carton, the man who ultimately dies for Darnay, is ready enough to "hate the fellow" (bk. 2, chap. 5, p. 79).

Less than a month after the last chapter of *A Tale of Two Cities* was published, James Fitzjames Stephen expressed his contempt for Darnay as a coward who "thought he had better live by his wits in London than have the responsibility of continuing to be a landowner in France."[1] Lawrence Frank, a recent interpreter, sees Charles almost as negatively as a self-deceiver, who "lives unknown in England, where he is 'no Marquis': unknown to his tenants in France; unknown to his wife; unknown, finally, to himself."[2] In 1970, the centennial year of Dickens' death, Sylvère Monod summed up the "unusually unanimous critical feeling against" Darnay, adding his own conviction that while Dickens may have identified with Darnay, "lending him for instance his own leaning towards 'The Loadstone Rock'" of self-destructiveness, he did not give this character "more than .01 percent" of his own vitality.[3]

Although David Copperfield has not been criticized as severely, many readers find him uninteresting, and some, including George Orwell, have been upset by his class consciousness, especially as expressed in his attitudes toward the villain, Uriah Heep. A. H. Gomme writes:

> It is impossible at times to avoid a feeling of special pleading against him, of Dickens with a knife in Uriah. . . . It is made a

---

1. James Fitzjames Stephen, "*A Tale of Two Cities*," *Saturday Review* (17 December 1859): 742.
2. Lawrence Frank, "Dickens' *A Tale of Two Cities:* The Poetics of Impasse," *American Imago* 36 (1979): 231.
3. Sylvère Monod, "Dickens's Attitudes in *A Tale of Two Cities*," in *Dickens Centennial Essays*, ed. Ada Nisbet and Blake Nevius, (Berkeley: University of California Press, 1971), p. 177. Monod cites condemnations of Charles by John Gross, K. J. Fielding, and Edgar Johnson.

point against him that not only does he pretend to a humility which in truth he does not own, but that he has a coarse accent and drops his aitches. . . . That . . . snobbery in Dickens as well as in David . . . becomes really vicious in the scene in which David is obsessed by Heep's physical repulsiveness.[4]

Sounding a bit like Sergeant Buzfuz addressing the jury in the famous case of Bardell versus Pickwick, even G. K. Chesterton, that confirmed Bozoliter, expresses sad disappointment at David's Prince Hal dismissals of all the truly valuable and "absurd" people in his life:

> We should have thought more of David Copperfield (and also of Charles Dickens) if he had endeavoured for the rest of his life, by conversation and comfort, to bind up the wounds of his old friends from the seaside. We should have thought more of David Copperfield (and also of Charles Dickens) if he had faced the possibility of going on till his dying day lending money to Mr. Wilkins Micawber. We should have thought more of David Copperfield (and also of Charles Dickens) if he had not looked upon the marriage to Dora merely as a flirtation, an episode which he survived and ought to survive. . . . I have a horrible feeling that David Copperfield will even send his aunt to Australia if she worries him too much about donkeys.[5]

Interestingly, Orwell, Gomme, and Chesterton have all three identified or perhaps even confused Dickens with his hero. There is nothing unusual about the belief that authors tend to empathize with their central characters, and in the case of Dickens this assumption has been long-standing as well as common. Readers have always been pleased to point out, either to Dickens himself or to one another, that Dickens' heroes, both David Copperfield and Charles Darnay, have the author's initials; and Phiz must have felt clever indeed when he quoted from the Maclise portrait of Dickens for one of his

---

4. A. H. Gomme, *Dickens* (London: Evans, 1971), p. 176. Orwell's criticism of David, along with his defense of Heep—"Even villains have sexual lives"—occurs in "Charles Dickens," in *Dickens, Dali and Others* (New York and London: Harcourt Brace Jovanovich, 1973), p. 41.

5. G. K. Chesterton, *Appreciations and Criticisms of the Works of Charles Dickens* (London: J. M. Dent & Sons, 1911), pp. 132–135.

Dombey and Son illustrations of Walter Gay.[6] Moreover, the reader frequently assumes not only the identification but also Dickens' ignorance of it and, at least before *Great Expectations*, his consequent inability to view the hero with any degree of critical objectivity.

Good criticism ought to resist such assumptions. Some authors are capable of identifying with and of fully creating only those characters who are like themselves, but Dickens, who as G. H. Lewes observed, could hallucinate himself into anyone's skin, is certainly not such a writer.[7] There is much of Dickens in every character he created, in Bill Sikes, Mrs. Gamp, Ralph Nickleby, and, indeed, even Uriah Heep, as well as in David Copperfield. And if, as it appears, we dislike David more than any of the other characters in his book (with the possible exceptions of the two women he marries), we ought not to begin, at least, with the complacent, self-congratulatory conviction that we are wiser, more perspicacious, more tolerant, more socially sensitive than the greatest, most observant, and most socially conscious of all novelists, whose essential tawdriness we have at last discovered. When we feel tempted to do so, we might do well to repeat Coleridge's golden rule of criticism: *Until you understand a writer's ignorance, presume yourself ignorant of his understanding.*

Nevertheless, while it is probably bad criticism to mistake the author for his faulty heroes, I am by no means certain that Dickens would have been disappointed with such a reading. For it is consistent with the aesthetics of the pious fraud discussed in the third chapter of this study, that just such a confusion between author and character was intended. It is indeed possible in light of these aesthetics that Dickens was laying a deep trap for us and hoping that our self-satisfaction and complacency might lead us to fall in. If so, we may de-

---

6. Most recently Michael Slater has argued in the "Introduction" to the Penguin Edition of *Nicholas Nickleby* that the hero of that novel is an idealized portrait of Dickens.

7. G. H. Lewes, "Dickens in Relation to Criticism," *Fortnightly Review* (Feb. 1872), pp. 141–54. Reprinted in *The Dickens Critics*, ed. George Ford and Lauriat Lane (Ithaca: Cornell University Press, 1961), p. 59.

cide we have an even better reason than before for disliking Dickens, but disliking Dickens is not the issue just now. We are concerned with his heroes, whom we resent, I am convinced, not because their feet of clay reveal the imperfections of their creator, who identifies too closely with them. Our anger is too nervous, too much like petulance for that explanation. We resent these innocuous characters because *we*, as readers, have been maddeningly forced to identify with them. The assumed name of the romantic hero of *A Tale of Two Cities* has the author's initials, all right, but his real name, Evrémonde, as critics have also discovered, is a pun on the word *everyman*.[8] I venture to guess that many of Dickens' readers, including, alas, this writer, resemble the stodgy Cambridge tutor Charles Darnay, and only a few are like the charming drunkard Sydney Carton; fewer still are pleased to acknowledge these facts.

Nor do I believe that we object to the identification with David for the reasons that are usually alleged against him, his snobbery and his final self-satisfaction. Readers are perfectly happy to identify with much more snobbish heroes in Thackeray and far more complacent characters in Trollope. Not many of us object very strenuously to being comfortable, and we can usually bear snobbery, when it is our own, with considerable equanimity. Certainly at least Chesterton could. The problem is not that Dickens lacks the objectivity to be critical of his heroes; quite the opposite: He sees in them the faults and disabilities that people in general, including, of course, his readers, want least to acknowledge in themselves—faults and disabilities that add up finally to a pervasive and crippling sense of undramatic unworthiness.

"The harlequins of life," Dickens wrote in *Bentley's Miscellany* in 1837, "are just ordinary men, to be found in no particular walk or degree, on whom a certain station, or particu-

---

8. See Robert Alter, "The Demons of History in Dickens' *Tale*," *Novel: A Forum of Fiction* 2 (1969): 138; and Elliot Gilbert, " 'To Awake from History': Carlyle, Thackeray, and *A Tale of Two Cities*," *Dickens Studies Annual* 12, ed. Michael Timko, Fred Kaplan, Edward Guiliano (New York: AMS Press, 1983), p. 259.

lar conjunction of circumstances, confers the magic wand."[9] In other words, Harlequin is like any one of Dickens' male readers, and he is fortunate rather than deserving. Columbine loves Harlequin rather than Pierrot, not because Harlequin deserves her more, but simply because she happens to love him more. As Richard Wardour, the man who fails to win the girl in Dickens and Collins' play *The Frozen Deep*, says of his successful rival, he has "got what the women call a lucky face."[10] Charles Darnay is "a rather handsome fellow," according to Sydney Carton, another rejected lover, "and I thought I should have been much the same sort of fellow, if I had had any luck" (bk. 2, chap. 5, pp. 81–82). The hero may live in relative poverty for a while, but, as Nicholas Nickleby's uncle bitterly exclaims, "There is some spell about that boy. . . . Circumstances conspire to help him. Talk of fortune's favours! What is even money to such Devil's luck as this?" (chap. 45, p. 569). Usually, however, and Nicholas is no exception, the hero's father was an aristocrat, a gentleman, or rich, or else the hero has great expectations of his own, which, in spite of Uncle Pumblechook's reassurances to the contrary, are not "Well deserved!" (chap. 19, p. 145). Or perhaps, like Young Martin Chuzzlewit or Walter Gay or Allan Woodcourt, he is born with the luck to survive fever or shipwreck; or, like David Copperfield, with a caul that will protect him from being "drowndead."

For all his good luck, however, the Dickensian hero is not a prepossessing character. He seldom gets any good lines to speak, and the truth about him seems to be that he is a rather dull and unthoughtful lover: Head over heels in love, he brings his beloved the present of a cookery book. Sharp-witted servants see through him at a glance and take advantage of the situation. True, the heroine loves him, but that, as we have seen, is a matter of luck. What Annie Strong sees in him is very difficult, not only for the disappointed Jack Mal-

---

9. Dickens, "The Pantomime of Life," 1: 295.
10. In *Under the Management of Mr. Charles Dickens: His Production of "The Frozen Deep,"* ed. Robert Louis Brannan (Ithaca: Cornell University Press, 1966), p. 130.

don, but for any reader to fathom. G. K. Chesterton, writing of *Dombey and Son*, registers his admiration for the imbecile Mr. Toots "by the somewhat violent expression that he is as good a lover as Walter Gay is a bad one. Florence surely deserved her father's scorn if she could prefer Gay to Toots."[11] When we learn that Biddy has forgotten Pip and come to her senses in time to marry the worthier Joe Gargery, we remember, perhaps, that Mary should not have been waiting for Martin Chuzzlewit when Tom Pinch was around and that Agnes Wickfield should not have been still ready for David Copperfield in the nineteenth monthly number. Certainly David knows it:

> I could not forget that the [sisterly] feeling with which she now regarded me had grown up in my own free choice and course. That if she had ever loved me with another love—and I sometimes thought the time was when she might have done so—I had cast it away. . . . What I might have done, I had not done, and what Agnes was to me, I and her own noble heart had made her. (P. 700)

None of this is especially flattering to the reader who has been tricked into identifying with this hero, but what is more depressing is the burden of guilt the hero carries about with him for having succeeded in spite of his unworthiness, or for some other equally frustrating reason. Every critic talks about the hero's guilt in *Great Expectations*, but the motif began much earlier in Dickens. Mr. Jingle of *Pickwick Papers* is a scoundrel who comes to see the error of his ways. Harry Maylie of *Oliver Twist*, who may have been a projection of Dickens in love with his recently dead sister-in-law (he is exactly Dickens' age, as Rose is Mary Hogarth's), is so bound up with scruples that he has to give up his hopeful career to feel qualified for Rose's love. In the next novel Nicholas Nickleby develops a set of scruples almost as complicated as his sentence structure, and just in time nearly to prevent his marriage to Madeline Bray:

---

11. G. K. Chesterton, *Charles Dickens* (London: Methuen, 1906), p. 187.

How base would it be of me to take advantage of the circumstances which have placed her here, or of the slight service I was happily able to render her, and to seek to engage her affections when the result must be if I succeeded, that the brothers would be disappointed in their darling wish of establishing their own child, and that I must seem to hope to build my fortunes on their compassion for the young creature whom I had so meanly and unworthily entrapped, turning her very gratitude and warmth of heart to my own purpose and account, and trading in her misfortunes [phew!]. . . . I doubt whether I have not done wrong even now. (Chap. 61, pp. 794-95)

At the other end of Dickens' career John Harmon experiences similar scruples in regard to Bella Wilfer, and Eugene Wrayburn harbors truly guilty intentions concerning Lizzie Hexam. As he hovers about her, Eugene tells Mortimer Lightwood, who represents his conscience, that "invisible insects of diabolical activity swarm in this place. I am tickled and twitched all over. Mentally, I have now committed a burglary under the meanest circumstances, and the myrmidons of justice are at my heels" (bk. 1, chap. 13, p. 165). Before the chapter is over he has expanded the guilt to include "three burglaries, two forgeries, and a midnight assassination" (p. 168). And when his conscience finally gets at him in the form of Bradley Headstone's club, he feels even worse.

Indeed the hero's guilt has been a constant throughout Dickens' career. Young Martin Chuzzlewit has plenty to trouble his conscience as soon as he goes back to Eden and develops one. Walter Gay remains spotless, but according to the original plans for *Dombey and Son*, he was supposed to have become corrupted by the world of commerce. Ebenezer Scrooge was a young lover before getting lost in that world, and so was Ralph Nickleby, whose guilt at a failure of love, like that of Bill Sikes, leads finally to the noose.

Sikes is a murderer, and Ralph is an obvious villain, but the guilt some Dickens' heroes experience is vaguer and more difficult to explain. Walter Wilding, the hero of *No Thoroughfare*, a collaboration with Wilkie Collins, discovers that he owes his comfortable position in life to the lucky circumstance of having been mistakenly exchanged for another infant. He says that he has "innocently got the inheritance of another man,"[12] a man unknown to him, but Wilding dies, nevertheless, of the resulting guilt. The guilt is even vaguer in the case of Arthur Clennam of *Little Dorrit*, who merely suspects that his modest inheritance was founded on some injustice his parents may have performed. Indefinite but powerful, his guilt is enough to cripple Arthur psychologically:

> There was the subject seldom absent from his mind, the question what he was to do henceforth in life; to what occupation he should devote himself, and in what direction he had best seek it. He was far from rich, and every day of indecision and inaction made his inheritance a source of greater anxiety to him. As often as he began to consider how to increase this inheritance, or to lay it by, so often his misgiving that there was some one with an unsatisfied claim upon his justice, returned; and that alone was a subject to outlast the longest walk. (Bk. 1, chap. 16, p. 183)

Eventually this vague guilt becomes so oppressive that Clennam, in a self-destructive flurry of action, succeeds both in impoverishing himself and being thrown into prison as a result of investing his own and the firm's money in a fraudulent scheme.

It is this kind of guilt, I believe, that readers most resent, for it stirs uneasy feelings of unworthiness, complicated by social and psychological reverberations. It reminds the fortunate readers of the dark side of having been born lucky, of being Oliver Twist rather than Little Dick, Rose Maylie rather than Nancy, or of occupying a social station somewhat closer to that of "your Majesty" in *Bleak House* than to that of Jo, the dead crossing-sweeper.

The social dimension of this feeling of guilt is addressed most directly, perhaps, in the case of the character with whom we began this discussion of unsatisfactory heroes, Charles Darnay of *A Tale of Two Cities*. For Charles is lucky not only in the ways for which Sydney Carton envies him. He is also

---

12. *Christmas Stories* (London: Oxford University Press, 1956), p. 561.

Hablot Browne, "Arthur Clennam [*right*] at Mr. John Chivery's Tea Table," 1857, from *Little Dorrit*. Courtesy of the University of California at Riverside Library.

lucky to have been born the son of a French aristocrat rather than a starving peasant, to be the child of the rapist's twin rather than of the rapist's victim. In an earlier draft of book 3, chapter 10, Charles' luck was even more clearly expressed, for instead of the rape, there was a false marriage, the kind of situation that might have led to the birth of an illegitimate child, an Ishmael, to contrast with the heir of the legitimate marriage. People of delicate conscience suffer from this hereditary guilt—for living while someone else is dead; for being comfortable while someone else is an outcast; for being loved while a brother or a sister is rejected. In the case of Charles Evrémonde, the luck of this guilty, or at least undeserved, birth is reemphasized at the moment marked for his own death, when his look-alike, very much unbidden, dies in his place.

Moreover, Charles feels guilty for specific crimes of omission, which may also apply to and bother a reader with an active social conscience. Charles has never properly renounced his evil inheritance in France, although he always meant to; like Dickens and the blacking warehouse incident, he has never confessed his shame even to his wife; and he has found himself powerless "to execute the last request of my dear mother's lips, and obey the last look of my dear mother's eyes, which implored me to have mercy and to redress" (bk. 2, chap. 9, p. 117). "What I have left to call my own," Charles' mother had told Dr. Manette, "I will make it the first charge of his life to bestow, with the compassion and lamenting of his dead mother, on this injured family, if the sister can be discovered" (bk. 3, chap. 10, p. 314). Charles does not fulfill this charge, but it is not entirely accurate to say that since he cannot or at least does not discover the sister, Madame Defarge, she discovers him instead. Charles is drawn to return to France, and to face the obvious danger there, not entirely for the reasons he states—the desire to save the innocent servant and the patriotic ambition to moderate the fury of the revolution—but because, like Arthur Clennam of *Little Dorrit*, he needs, or rather thinks he needs, to be punished. So, very likely, do the rest of us, but it's little wonder if we resent being told so.

David Copperfield makes things even harder on the identifying reader than Charles Darnay does. For one thing, since we encounter David first as an engaging child, living in an idyllic house and served by two adoring females, we are eager to share his experiences. In contrast Charles Darnay is introduced as an all but condemned felon, soon to be "shamefully mangled," his body "butchered and torn asunder." Entering the courtroom with the obscenely curious Jerry Cruncher, we see Charles first from the perspective of the Old Bailey mob, and we are told that "whatever gloss the various spectators put upon the interest, according to their several arts and powers of self-deceit, the interest was, at the root of it, Ogreish" (bk. 2, chap. 2, pp. 58–59). There is no description of him as a child until much later in the novel when Doctor Manette's narrative is read in the French court, where Charles is once again in danger of condemnation and mutilation. Manette describes the child who is to grow up to be this international prisoner at the bar as "a pretty boy from two to three years old," innocently accepting responsibility for all the sins of his ancestors (bk. 3, chap. 10, p. 314). Readers have usually and understandably preferred to identify with the brilliant wastrel Sydney Carton.

There are no comparable warnings in the case of David Copperfield. Indeed the first five numbers of his novel, ending with David's rebirth at Dover, provide what might be a textbook example in a creative writing class on achieving reader identification, as, after being graciously invited to join David's happiness, we are made to suffer familiar persecutions with him, to share in his grief and seemingly hopeless sufferings, and finally to triumph heroically with him when Aunt Betsey threatens to tread upon Jane Murdstone's bonnet. Hardly anyone objects to David in the first five numbers. Even George Bernard Shaw grudged him "tolerable as a child."[13] Moreover, David's ambiguous gender, concerning which I shall say more later on, renders him accessible to readers of

---

13. George Bernard Shaw, "Epistle Dedicatory," *Man and Superman* in *The Bodley Head Bernard Shaw* (London: Max Reinhardt, 1971), 2: 522.

both sexes, who find him at the same time manly and sensitive, capable of an innocent romantic attachment not only to Little Em'ly but also to Steerforth.

Although the young David is irresistible, he grows up to become at least as problematic as Charles Darnay. We want him to win all the girls and women in the novel, even the eldest Miss Larkins, but we don't feel he really deserves any of them. And so far as guilt is concerned, Arthur Clennam, Charles Darnay, Pip, and even Eugene Wrayburn feel comparably innocent. David blames himself for having indirectly caused Mr. Mell to lose his position and for having facilitated Emily's seduction. He also feels guilty for distrusting Steerforth, the real culprit in both actions. He is in constant anxiety at the prospect of being found out by servants and of being exposed by Uriah Heep. In his marriage David sees himself as playing the spider's part, lying in wait for Dora's faults, disciplining her to death in the manner of a Murdstone, and perhaps ultimately, as Chesterton would have it, of causing her death by unconsciously wishing it. If so, then it is only just to note that he has also wished for his own early death because he believes that some crime or crimes unspecified have since rendered him unworthy of salvation. "I should have been more fit for Heaven," he says when he sees the infant brother who has replaced him in his mother's arms, "than I have ever been since" (p. 94). If David feels overly complacent at the end of his story, he has either worked through or put aside a great quantity of guilt along the way. *David Copperfield*, as Shaw recognized as early as 1889, "is a book of pain, doubt, anxiety, and unfulfillment."[14]

Perhaps David's existential guilt lacks the theological quality of Charles Darnay's—David's problem is not, so far as I can understand it, a question of original sin—but, although *David Copperfield* has usually been regarded as Dickens' most autobiographical and psychological novel, the guilt does not lack a social dimension. Much of David's guilt stems from the

---

14. From a paper written during November 1889 and published for the first time in *Shaw on Dickens*, ed. Laurence and Quinn, p. 17.

desperate and, of course, futile attempt, discussed earlier, to escape death by becoming a gentleman. The motives of Dickens' heroes are always wonderfully mixed, and even the least of them, take Nicholas Nickleby, are more complex than the central characters of so-called realistic novels. David is no exception. But certainly his infatuation with Steerforth, which dominates the first half of the novel, is at least partly motivated by Steerforth's cool gentility.

> I didn't think Miss Creakle equal to Little Em'ly in point of beauty, and I didn't love her (I didn't dare); but I thought her a young lady of extraordinary attractions, and in point of gentility not to be surpassed. When Steerforth, in white trousers, carried her parasol for her, I felt proud to know him; and believed that she could not choose but adore him with all her heart. Mr. Sharp and Mr. Mell were both notable personages in my eyes; but Steerforth was to them what the sun was to two stars. (P. 79)

Eventually, he will defer to Steerforth also in the matter of Emily. One critic, John O. Jordan, argues that David gives Emily to Steerforth, as a brother might give his sister in marriage, as an unconscious attempt to buy his way into Steerforth's class.[15] It is certainly true that David, almost as obviously as Mrs. Nickleby in the case of the sexual threat against Kate, chooses blithely to ignore the plentiful warnings about Steerforth's intentions just as he chooses to excuse Steerforth's frequent expressions of contempt for the servant class from which David himself partly springs.

As we have seen, moreover, it is Steerforth who encourages David to pursue the genteel career of a proctor. He thus introduces David to the infatuation which is to replace him in the second half of the novel, the gentleman proctor's daughter, to whom David hopelessly loses his heart, not "in a minute" *after* seeing her, as he tells us, but, in fact, some

---

15. John O. Jordan, "The Social Sub-text of *David Copperfield*," in *Dickens Studies Annual* 14, ed. Michael Timko, Fred Kaplan and Edward Guiliano (New York: AMS Press, 1985), p. 69. Jordan further argues that David expects to get Rosa Dartle for himself in this exchange of sisters (pp. 69–70).

minutes before they even set eyes on one another or hear one another's names. It happens in Spenlow's elegant garden as David is approaching the house for the first time:

> There was a lovely garden to Mr. Spenlow's house; and though that was not the best time of the year for seeing a garden, it was so beautifully kept that I was quite enchanted. There was a charming lawn, there were clusters of trees, and there were perspective walks that I could just distinguish in the dark, arched over with trellis-work on which shrubs and flowers grew in the growing season. "Here Miss Spenlow walks by herself," I thought. "Dear me!"
> We went into the house, which was cheerfully lighted up, and into a hall where there were all sorts of hats, caps, greatcoats, plaids, gloves, whips, and walking-sticks. "Where is Dora?" said Mr. Spenlow to the servant. "Dora," I thought. "What a beautiful name!" (P. 333)

No one can doubt the sincerity of David's subsequent impulsive attachment to Dora Spenlow, any more than one would suspect the innocent David of craftily cultivating Steerforth's friendship, but it remains that both these guilt-laden relationships began, not with David's attraction to Dora or Steerforth themselves but to the gentility they represented to him, the gentility that, as I argued earlier, he imagines will somehow protect him from death.

This complicated, guilt-laden character may seem to the reader of this study to be at a far remove from the mindless Harlequin of nineteenth-century pantomime and to have even less in common with his ancestor, Arlecchino, the roguish servant of commedia dell'arte or even with his cousin on the contemporary French stage, whom Théophile Gautier describes as the embodiment of love, wit, mobility, daring, all the shining vices: Harlequin, "with the phiz of a monkey and the body of a snake, with his black mask, his motley diamond-shaped patches, and his glittering spangles."[16]

Perhaps a residue of the wickedness in the character of

---

16. Quoted in Thelma Niklaus, *Harlequin Phoenix: or The Rise and Fall of a Bergamask Rogue* (London: Bodley Head, 1956), p. 14.

Harlequin accounts partly for the guilt in the Dickensian hero. Usually on the English stage the character who would be transformed to Harlequin was the equivalent of the spotless hero of melodrama, but there were pantomimes, especially in the 1830s, where he was derived from such questionable characters as Guy Fawkes and Peeping Tom.[17] With this in mind, we should recall that Dickens' first Harlequin was the roguish Jingle. More frequently the character who becomes Harlequin in the pantomime is guilty of some less shameful crime than that of Tom of Coventry's but one that nevertheless requires serious expiation. Thus, as the action is described in the synopsis to Charles Farley's *Harlequin and the Ogress; or, the Sleeping Beauty of the Wood*, a Grimaldi vehicle: "The Princess awakes, is enamoured of the Prince, who, in his ecstasy at the sight of her, loses the Magic Flower, given him by his Good Genius, for which he is doomed to range with his Princess as Harlequin and Columbine until he can restore the lost gift."[18] And in *Harlequin and Mother Goose* (1806), which many regard as the first significant Regency pantomime, Colin consents to the killing of the goose and must wander the world in expiation until he recovers the golden egg.

The ranging that David Copperfield, without his Princess, must perform after the deaths of Dora and Steerforth probably owes more to *Childe Harold* and Carlyle's "Centre of Indifference" than to the harlequinade, although after Byron the harlequinade frequently took the form of a world tour, which often served as a means of expiation. David's wanderings, which include, like the Ancient Mariner's, the telling of "a Story, with a purpose growing, not remotely, out of my own experience" (p. 699), presumably enable him to overcome his

---

17. *Harlequin and Guy Fawkes; or, The Fifth of November* (London: W. Kenneth, 1835). *Harlequin Peeping Tom of Coventry.* Manuscript in the Lord Chamberlain's Collection at the British Library. Performed at Covent Garden, 1837. Perhaps Joyce, the writer after Dickens whose art may owe the most to pantomime, was aware of a later version of this panto.

18. Charles Farley, *Harlequin and the Ogress; or, the Sleeping Beauty of the Wood* (London: John Miller, 1822).

grief as well as his guilt, and they prepare him to learn the essential lesson of his life, the disciplining of his heart. The specifics of David's course of study under Aunt Betsey were detailed earlier in my discussion of the Benevolent Agent, but it is now the time to note that the pattern of such an expiation and education in Dickens frequently involves traveling, a miraculous escape from death, and sometimes the intervention of a supernatural force. Joe Willet, Martin Chuzzlewit, Walter Gay, Allan Woodcourt, and perhaps Edwin Drood—all cross the seas and have their brushes with death. Arthur Clennam, who has been to China, nearly dies at home, as do Pip, John Harmon, and the peripatetic Eugene Wrayburn, all of whom nearly drown in the Thames. Pickwick, Gabriel Grub, Nicholas Nickleby, Kit Nubbles, and Ebenezer Scrooge get, at least, to see a good deal of England, as well as some other things they had not counted on. The harlequinade, as Dickens noted in "A Curious Dance Round a Curious Tree," is full of deaths that do not kill;[19] it is always governed, moreover, by supernatural and irrational forces; and it never stops moving for an instant.

But the guilt of the hero had become a mild business in the English pantomime and might, at the most, have provided a hint to Dickens. After Grimaldi there were no "shining vices," and the spirit of mischief had clearly passed to Clown and Pantaloon. Harlequin still retained his magic bat or slapstick, which permitted him to make nifty escapes when cornered by his adversaries and at the same time to make loud noises that cued the stagehands for lightning-quick changes in scenery so that he could find himself in an entirely new locale and a completely different situation, free of the consequences of the preceding action and "innocently" ready to plunge into new complications. Harlequin also continued to win the love of Columbine, although this part of the story was becoming more and more difficult to understand, especially by young boys in the audience, for, beginning in the 1830s, he

---

19. *Household Words*, 17 January 1852, p. 385.

Harlequin, from a Juvenile Drama Sheet, circa 1830.

was literally losing his gender.[20] The gymnast who played Harlequin in the comic business was almost always male, but the young lover of the opening, from whom he was transformed by the Benevolent Agent, was more and more frequently played by a woman, the "Principal Boy," as she is still called in modern pantomimes. He/she or she/he is brave, cheerful, and enthusiastic, but Harlequin's essentially male energy, which, as the bat symbolized, was clearly erotic, and which had, after all, motivated Columbine's rebellion against her father and the hierarchy in the first place, has been lost and was already fast disappearing even during Dickens' youth.

The role of Principal Boy, or rather the stage tradition that justified it, was hardly a chaste one. The point of putting an actress in men's clothing, at least since Samuel Pepys ogled one in 1661, was to show her legs,[21] and when Peg Woffington played "breeches parts" in the eighteenth century no one in the audience forgot for a moment that she was a sexually exciting woman. It was the same with Madame Vestris in the extravaganzas of the mid-nineteenth century. By the end of the Victorian period the Principal Boys of pantomime were dressed, or rather undressed, and frequently even padded, so as to emphasize their womanliness. Cross-dressing seems always to have been a turn-on for the English. Pantomime Principal Boys, however, were very rare before the 1850s, and although more and more women were being cast as the hero, those, like Elizabeth Poole, who ventured to take the role in the 1830s and 1840s, appear to have been relatively modest. Like the actresses Dickens had seen impersonating such characters as Oliver Twist, Smike, Jo, and Paul Dombey in stage adaptations of his novels, they were playing unsexed boys rather than doubly sexed women.

20. Elizabeth Poole is the most famous of the 1830s cross-dressed heroes, but Eliza Povey played the hero of *Jack and the Beanstalk* as early as 1819.
21. On 28 October 1661 Pepys wrote of an actress in male attire that she "had the best legs that ever I saw, and I was very well pleased with it." *The Diary of Samuel Pepys,* ed. Robert Latham and William Matthews (Berkeley and Los Angeles: University of California Press, 1970), 2: 203.

Elizabeth Poole as the Hero of *Puss in Boots*, 1832. Courtesy of David Mayer III.

Certainly such a character no longer posed a sexual threat to the hierarchical society he used to stand on its ear, and he must have become somewhat of a puzzle even to himself. Thus, if Dickens' hero suffers from an identity problem, so does his model from the pantomime. A modern audience sometimes squirms a bit when a busty Robin Hood sings a tender lovesong to Maid Marian, and, at least on opening night, the actresses themselves sometimes have a hard time keeping straight faces as they look soulfully into one another's eyes.

We have already spoken of how the child David Copperfield's sexual ambiguity aids in the business of reader identification. I suspect it has also a good deal to do with the negative way he is frequently viewed as an adult. It is even possible to be uncomfortably confused about him when, as a boy, he is delighted to be "cherished" by Steerforth "as a kind of plaything in my room" (p. 81), although one must, of course, agree with Sylvère Monod, who concludes, after noting evidence of David's effeminate character, that "Dickens cannot be held to have intended to hint at the existence of unnatural feelings—not to speak of intercourse—between David and Steerforth."[22] Nevertheless David must have been troubled by his sexual identity from the time he heard the story of his aunt's disappointment about Betsey Trotwood Copperfield. His father, lying in the nearby cemetery, is a powerful force on his imagination, but before the appearance of Murdstone, David was brought up in a home without a male role model. When he arrives in Dover to "make another beginning" (p. 185), he is wrapped in nondescript female clothing and given a unisex name, Trotwood. Later he recalls a boyhood of infatuations and schoolboy adventures at Canterbury, but it is as difficult to believe in his glorious pugilistic victory over the butcher (p. 232) as in Oliver Twist's thrashing of Noah Claypole. One has only to look at the illustrations of the girlishly slight figure of this hero who is called Doady by

22. Monod, *Dickens the Novelist*, p. 324.

his wife and Daisy by his best friend. When he slaps Uriah rather than punches him, David is clearly in character, and we are not overly surprised when Heep chooses not to return the blow. In fact many of the men and all the servants treat David with disdainful condescension. James Kincaid comments on what he takes to be David's inability to deal with any real crisis when one forces its way into his dream world: "His absolute impotence in the face of a real threat should escape no one. He is simply unable to act in a real situation."[23] But these curious bouts of paralysis in moments of crisis, as when Micawber is exploding Heep, or when Rosa Dartle is berating Emily, or during the storm at Yarmouth, are less difficult to understand if we think of David, not as hero, but as Principal Boy, a girl in boy's costume.[24] Indeed, as a contemporary, Margaret Oliphant, wrote concerning all the Dickens heroes, but with special reference to David Copperfield, "Homebred and sensitive, much impressed by feminine influences . . . their courage is of the order of courage which belongs to women."[25] Amiable Prince Turveydrop, whose "little, innocent, feminine manner" appeals to Esther Summerson of *Bleak House* (chap. 14, p. 190), indicates Dickens' continued preference for the "unmanly" hero.

V. C. Clinton-Baddeley noted in 1963 that the part of the Principal Boy "has been occasionally played by a man—for instance the equestrian Aladdin at the Royal Amphitheatre in 1830 and 1833, and notably in *Sleeping Beauty* at Drury Lane in 1912, 1913, and 1914. [And there have been other more recent experiments, as well, as in *Cinderella* at the Palladium in 1985.] But it never really works. It is small good trying to

---

23. James Kincaid, "The Darkness of *David Copperfield*," *Dickens Studies* 1 (1965): 70.

24. A Danish silent film version of *Hamlet* (Asta Films, 1920), which I have been assured is not intended to be comic, has a woman in the title role and suggests that the reason for Hamlet's procrastination is that he/she is really a disguised girl. This fact also explains Hamlet's problems with Ophelia and the evident attraction of Horatio.

25. Margaret Oliphant, "Charles Dickens," *Blackwood's* 77 (1855): 451.

make sense of pantomime."[26] One is tempted, nevertheless.[27] For the question as to why the hero of romance is so insipid has to be more important than Hazlitt allowed,[28] or than Mario Praz, who concluded that Dickens and his contemporaries, living in a *Biedermeier* age, opted for the picturesque rather than the sublime because of their "dislike [of] the melodramatic and the heroic."[29] With Dickens, Tennyson, Disraeli, and Carlyle as its chief spokesmen, no more melodramatic or hero-hungry age has ever existed.

But what does it mean, after all, when the central male character of such an age's most popular theatrical forms, melodrama and pantomime, is presented as stupid or is played by a young woman, or when the period's major poem, *In Memoriam*, is supposed by an early reviewer to have been written by the grieving widow of a military man? Nor is David Copperfield the only effeminate male narrator of a Victorian novel. There are also the girlish narrators of *Guy Livingstone* and *John Halifax, Gentleman*, both of whom join David and Tennyson in the supinely adoring celebration of a powerful, manly hero. There is also Lockwood, the foppish narrator who tells the demonic story of Heathcliff; and, in America, the vaguely homosexual Ishmael, who writes the tragedy of the Promethean Ahab. The fascination that all these narrators express for their opposites or alter egos does not bespeak dislike for the heroic, although Steerforth and the others are frequently ambiguous characters.

26. V. C. Clinton-Baddeley, *Some Pantomime Pedigrees* (London: The Society for Theatre Research, 1963), p. 20.
27. The best attempt has been by David Mayer III, who offers an explanation in Marxist-Freudian terms. "The Sexuality of Pantomime," *Theatre Quarterly* 4 (1974): 55–64.
28. Hazlitt's explanation, offered in his playful essay, "Why Heroes of Romance are Insipid," is that otherwise "they would no longer be those 'faultless monsters' which it is understood that they must be to fill their part in the drama." *The Complete Works of William Hazlitt*, ed. P. P. Howe, 21 vols. (London and Toronto: J. M. Dent, 1933), 17: 247.
29. Mario Praz, *The Hero in Eclipse in Victorian Fiction*, trans. Angus Davidson (London, New York, Toronto: Oxford University Press, 1956), pp. 162–63.

Far from rejecting the heroic, these works are trying desperately to believe in it, albeit with only limited success. Another Tennysonian hero who may cast light on this problem is Sir Galahad, the only character from the *Idylls* whose victory is unqualified. Galahad, like the hero of pantomime, is pure as a maid.[30] Feminine Dickensian heroes, according to Mrs. Oliphant once again, "are spotless in their thoughts, their intentions, and wishes. Into those dens of vice and unknown mysteries, whither the lordly Pelham may penetrate without harm, and which Messrs Pendennis and Warrington frequent that they may see 'life,' David Copperfield could not enter without pollution. In the very heart and soul of him, this young man . . . is pure."[31]

If maidenly purity is a requirement for heroism, then the hero must be something of a girl, and not only a girl, but a virgin of the sort the nineteenth century fantasized, and perhaps even one lacking in sexual energy of any sort. Needless to say, this is an unrealistic expectation if the hero is intended as a model for readers eager to lead a heroic life in the real world. Another contemporary reader, James Fitzjames Stephen, who prided himself on a tough-minded determination to live practically and to improve society through the established system, had no patience for Dickens' "feminine, irritable, noisy mind, which is always clamouring and shrieking for protection and guidance."[32]

But the resentment we feel toward the Dickensian central character, whom we are obviously intended to identify with, may go farther even than this. It is similar to the resentment that Tristram, Pelleus, and the other failed knights of the

---

30. In the Ur-poem to *The Holy Grail, Sir Galahad* (1842), Galahad calls himself "a maiden knight," and claims "My strength is as the strength of ten, / Because my heart is pure." An interesting article by Muriel Whitaker, "The Boy's Sir Launcelot," shows how Malory's adulterous knight was laundered in Victorian versions so as to make him "the very model of a modern English gentleman" (*Litir Newsletter* 5:1, 3).

31. Oliphant, "Charles Dickens," pp. 451–52.

32. James Fitzjames Stephen, "Mr. Dickens as a Politician," *Saturday Review* 3 (3 January 1857): 9.

Idylls express toward King Arthur. Unable to live up to standards that would make them better than they are, they bitterly choose to become far worse than they might have been. Even if the expectation were not unrealistic, isn't castration too high a price to pay for heroism? And where does an unsexed hero leave Columbine, who in the old story defied the hierarchy because of her passion for the phallic Harlequin, a passion which, though chaste enough, was unambiguously heterosexual. No wonder Orwell makes excuses for the villain's lust, and Chesterton cannot understand why the heroine does not give herself to the Clown.

7

Columbine: A Pure Woman

> Agnes is the most disagreeable of his heroines, the real legless angel of Victorian romance.
> —George Orwell

> Decidedly the most seventh rate heroine ever produced by a first rate artist.
> —George Bernard Shaw

Columbine's is not a grateful part in the pantomime, and, unlike Harlequin's, it never was. Her preference for Colin over the Squire motivates the action of *Mother Goose* and many another panto opening, but her rebellion, such as it is, is not a very complex business, and she is too frequently willing, albeit with a soulful look at her lover, to sacrifice herself at her father's command. Madeline Bray of *Nicholas Nickleby*, who is prepared to marry a septuagenarian miser so that her sybaritic father can have his comforts, is perhaps Dickens' purest version of the character in the panto who gets transformed into Columbine and spends the rest of the evening in a long dress, skimming across the stage, alternately comforted by Harlequin and terrified by all the others. Columbine is the object of the harlequinade chase, the central object for the three or four comics who surround her, but her principal business is simply to be vulnerable and pretty.

Early Dickensian heroines, even those obviously modeled on the author's idealized memory of his dead sister-in-law, Mary Hogarth, do and stand for little more than such a Columbine does and represents. The religious values that, as we shall see, J. Hillis Miller and Alexander Welsh ascribe to Agnes Wickfield of *David Copperfield* are apparent as early as Little Nell, but, generally speaking, these heroines—Rose,

Kate, Madeline, Barbara, Dolly, Emma, Mary, and Florence—are primarily long-suffering victims who have little to distinguish themselves but their innocence, their loyalty, and their endless willingness to sacrifice their own happiness. If I am not mistaken, the general reader may have had to think for a moment just now to remind himself which of the novels some of them come from. In his account of the pantomime in *Pickwick Papers*, Shaw wrote that "the only figure of the conventional Harlequinade which Dickens left as he found it . . . is the columbine. There are several attempts at her—Arabella Allen, the pretty housemaid, Emily Wardle, &c; but each seems the most hopeless doll in the set until we turn to the other and pronounce her worse." Shaw writes further of Dickens that this "failure [to create an interesting heroine] is significant of his cardinal disability as a novelist."[1]

Criticism that regards the Dickensian heroine, first, as the hero's redeemer, his angel of the hearthside,[2] and, more recently, as the victim of a patriarchial society from which the hero also suffers, have made the heroines more interesting. Nell, Esther, and Amy, according to the authors of a recent work of feminist criticism, "are not paragons but examples of thwarted potential. Rather than representing the [naive] solution [to the *hero's* problems], they underscore the need for a reformation of the basic assumptions about sexual identity and sexual roles."[3] Of course one need not adopt this either-or position, especially with the later heroines: It could be argued, for instance, that Esther Summerson of *Bleak House* has to redeem herself or be redeemed, that she needs to gain self-confidence and a sense of self-worth before she can do much good for others,[4] and that Bella Wilfer of *Our Mutual Friend* must be freed from her bondage to the social system and its

---

1. *Shaw on Dickens*, p. 24.
2. See especially Alexander Welsh, *The City of Dickens* (Oxford: Oxford University Press, 1971).
3. Richard Barickman, Susan MacDonald, and Myra Stark, *Corrupt Relations: Dickens, Thackeray, Trollope, Collins, and the Victorian Sexual System* (New York: Columbia University Press, 1982), p. 77.
4. See, for instance, my own *The Metaphysical Novel in England and America: Dickens, Bulwer, Hawthorne, Melville* (Berkeley and Los Angeles: University of California Press, 1978), p. 199ff.

Columbine, from a Juvenile Drama Sheet, circa 1830.

worldview before she can be of any use in the business of unburying John Harmon. She must become a person herself before she can help him recover his own misplaced identity.

The only "heroines" in the early works whose personal difficulties are obviously germane to the thematic problems of the novels in which they appear are the "fallen" women—Nancy, Alice Marwood, and Edith Dombey. Nancy is a victim of the same indifference and exploitations that threaten Oliver and destroy Bill Sikes. Edith and Alice, the cousins from *Dombey and Son*, are both commodities in a commercial world, to be sold and bought like James Carker, the wage-slave who is attracted to each of them, and they share his bitter resentment. Dickens is sometimes criticized for his failure to forgive the sexual transgressions of these women, but in fact they are treated no more brutally and sometimes rather more gently than the men with whom they are associated.

A similar heroine in *David Copperfield* is Little Em'ly, who, as I have argued, shares David's preoccupation with death and believes even more desperately than he does in the saving power of gentility. Dickens, as with the fallen women of *Dombey and Son*, seems incapable of forgiving her completely, although, once again, Steerforth is punished more inexorably. But what distinguishes Emily from the earlier Dickens women is the ritualistic expiation she must undergo to win back even her modest, childless position in the novel's moral world. Nancy has plenty of goodness left in her and is able, therefore, to look upward at the moment of her death, and Alice Marwood is inspired by Harriet Carker to adopt a better frame of mind. Against the strong urgings of those modern feminist readers who want revenge, Edith is at least trying to achieve grace for herself by forgiving Dombey. But Emily is treated with more seriousness even than Dickens was used to according his guilty heroes at this stage of his career. After her escape from Littimer, she must recover from a deathly illness, like Martin Chuzzlewit, and, like Walter Gay, she must survive a symbolic drowning:

> "The fire was afore her eyes, and the roarings in her ears; and there was no to-day, nor yesterday, nor yet to-morrow; but

everything in her life as ever had been, or as ever could be, and everything as never had been, was a crowding on her all at once." (P. 621)

In the 1840s either one of these ordeals would have been enough to redeem a guilty hero, but Emily's symbolic rebirth is not so easily achieved. To absolve herself of the stain of her unworthy ambition to attain gentility, she must unwish the fairy-tale bad wish to become a lady. She must teach the Italian children who befriend her to call her "Fisherman's daughter" instead of "Pretty lady" (p. 622); she must abjectly take "service to wait on travelling ladies at an inn" (p. 622) in France; and, after landing destitute in England, she must literally reverse David's heroic march to gentility when he walked from Murdstone and Grinby's in London to his aunt's house in Dover (p. 622).[5] No hero is put through so elaborate a symbolic ordeal until Pip, who also remains imperfectly forgiven, but several of the later heroines—Esther, Amy, Bella—must undergo similar ritualistic acts of contrition or regeneration. Emily begins this line, but although her redemption does not give her the power to save others, she represents a step beyond the earlier heroines, who are simply born with this power, and a step toward the later heroines, who ultimately achieve it.

David Copperfield is peopled with a greater number of sexually interesting women, perhaps, than any other Dickens novel. At least before she emigrates to Australia, Martha, the prostitute, is not seen in a sexual context, but this cannot be said of Miss Mowcher, the bawd, or of most of the other women, including the flirtatious daughter of Mr. Omer, the undertaker. Aunt Betsey has had a passionate involvement; David's landlady gives romantic advice; and Mrs. Micawber

---

5. Keith Carabine has written that "David's walk to Dover is as irrepressible an assertion of individuality and of the will to succeed as Heep's faith in his father's words, 'be 'umble Uriah . . . and you'll get on,' or Littimer's persistent worship of the god of 'respectability' " ("Reading *David Copperfield*," in *Reading the Victorian Novel: Detail into Form*, ed. Ian Gregor [London: Vision Press, 1980], p. 160).

keeps on having children. "Would you believe it. . . . Why, someun even made offers fur to marry . . . Missis Gummidge" (p. 744). Other widows, like Mrs. Steerforth and Mrs. Heep, are in love with their sons, and Clara Copperfield flirts with David before losing her heart to Murdstone. Rosa Dartle was Steerforth's mistress before Emily, and David is briefly in love with her. Indeed David, who is perhaps the ultimate Harlequin, is never out of love. His list includes Emily, Agnes, and Dora, not to mention Miss Shepherd, the eldest Miss Larkins, and, if he had dared, Miss Creakle. He regards even Peggotty as "a very handsome woman" (p. 14), and, of course, Peggotty does find a man who is willing. Nor are Emily, Martha, and Rosa Dartle the only women in the novel who are involved in seductions. From David's probably oedipal point of view, his mother is seduced by Murdstone, and he worries about Annie Strong's apparent weakness for her cousin Jack Maldon.

In the midst of all this sexuality Mrs. Strong is interesting to most readers only so long as she seems seduceable. Once she clears herself, Annie joins her friend Agnes Wickfield, according to most critics, as one of the great, sententious bores of literature. The trouble with Agnes is perhaps that she seems to be in so little trouble. Uriah Heep lusts after her, but, as she reassures David and the reader, there is no cause for concern. Agnes appears to be the ultimate instance of what the critic Barbara Hardy calls the heroine of "encapsulated virtue."[6] She is safer from Heep even than Nell is from Quilp, for she seems to lack the typical Columbine's tendency to panic and her mechanism for flight. As mentioned earlier, Dickens flirted with the idea of making Agnes the subject of a serious study of an alcoholic's daughter but he chose not to develop this strain yet. Consequently her self-possession, and the apparent absence in her of any psychological weaknesses, or at least any that her *author* seems to recognize, is

---

6. Barbara Hardy, *The Moral Art of Charles Dickens* (London: Athlone Press, 1970), p. 5.

surely what makes her so infuriating to readers. In love with David she rejoices in his marriage to another woman. Her patience with him as with her alcoholic father is maddeningly endless. She may be, as J. Hillis Miller writes, "a late example of that transposition of religious language into the realm of romantic love which began with the poets of courtly love," and David may have "that relation to Agnes which a devout Christian has to God, the creator of his selfhood, without whom he would be nothing,"[7] but where does such a strictly symbolic understanding of the character leave women readers, trained by habit to identify with the heroine of a novel, and for whom Agnes Wickfield seems to stand as a personal and wrong-headed reproach?

Indeed, the symbolic defense of Agnes by Miller, Welsh,[8] and others, although it constitutes intelligent, insightful criticism, tends only to increase resentment. Barbara Hardy's tone of impatient and justifiable anger at the American school of Dickensians is unmistakable when she dismisses the defense of Dickens' heroines "on the grounds that their identity is symbolic rather than realistic and related to fairy-tale or myth rather than to the imitation of life":

> It is obviously—very obviously—true that they are presented in fairy-tale and fabulous terms, but this only serves to draw attention to their sentimentality.[9]

Hardy goes on to compare the Dickens heroine unfavorably with the legitimate fairy-tale (and pantomime) heroine Cinderella. The choice is instructive. Of all the characters in fantasy literature, Cinderella is perhaps the one with whom girls find it easiest to identify. She is put-upon by a stepmother, and her unworthy siblings get all the advantages. And unlike Agnes Wickfield she is human enough to resent the treatment she receives. Cinderella longs to be loved, and

---

7. J. Hillis Miller, *Charles Dickens: The World of His Novels* (Cambridge, Mass.: Harvard University Press, 1958), p. 157.
8. Welsh, *The City of Dickens.*
9. Barbara Hardy, *Dickens: The Later Novels* (London: Longmans, 1968), p. 10.

her essential worth is immediately apparent to the only man in the story's world worth any real woman's having. In the pantomime, moreover, she has a father who loves her but is too weak to protect her from stepmother and the girls, and she has a comic servant, Buttons, an invention of the early nineteenth century, who does all the really dirty jobs around the house because he loves her hopelessly. As opposed to Annie Strong, who, like some of Dickens' best women readers, is married to a dull, old scholar in slippers, and in contrast to Agnes Wickfield, who after years of being slighted, is, like some other readers, still waiting for her used-up, androgynous hero to declare himself, Cinderella is wish-fulfillment personified. What I am arguing is that women dislike identifying with Dickens' heroines as much as men dislike identifying with his heroes, and that it is certainly *not* because these readers are *less* sentimental, *less* given to wish-fulfillment than Dickens. The reader of this study who is not laughing now may well be angry, and if so, I have provided an example of what I take Dickens' strategy to be. The glass slippers that Dickens sends around to his readers of both sexes are designed to pinch. His fiction is not intended to gratify the Cinderellas among us but to redeem the ugly sisters, and the first step in such a program has to be to convince them that they are not, in their present, unconverted state, all that could be desired.

Annie Strong and Agnes Wickfield are objectionable finally because the one is the spokeswoman in the novel and the other the great exemplar of the concept of the "disciplined heart," a theme discussed earlier from the point of view of the Benevolent Agent and the morality of the Dickensian (and Shakespearean) motif of the pious fraud. Now that we have introduced a consideration of sentimental wish-fulfillment and reader objection to a forced identification with the less attractive qualities of the heroes and heroines of Dickens, it may prove interesting to think once more about David's need to achieve maturity by disciplining his heart. How, in other words, is the reader likely to feel about the implied necessity of disciplining his or her own?

Until he achieves his disciplined heart, the lack of it is perhaps the most aggravating item in David's inventory of nagging guilt feelings. It is upsetting to the reader for several reasons. For one thing, David keeps harping on it, and, for another, we are not sure for a long time exactly what it is supposed to be. Once again, we are encouraged throughout most of the novel to assume that having a disciplined heart means to develop, like Tom Jones and Edward Waverley, some strength of character and independence of mind.

When Annie Strong introduces this concept of the disciplined heart, thanking her husband for having saved her "from the first mistaken impulse of my undisciplined heart" (p. 564), it appears that Dickens is encouraging this conventional interpretation. Certainly David at first draws this meaning from Annie's statement, especially when he sounds it together in his head with another of her pronouncements: "There can be no disparity in marriage like unsuitability of mind and purpose" (p. 567). If David had been what Aunt Betsey calls "a fine firm fellow" instead of a soft girl, he would not have been seduced by his infatuation for Dora, seduced almost as fatally and, as it seems at the time, as irrevocably as Little Em'ly was by Steerforth. Indeed, David has been a little soft from the beginning—he has not known how to control servants; he has allowed himself to be taken advantage of by Steerforth; and he has not been able yet to take his life properly into his own hands.

These are serious faults, but they are typical of the English hero before he reaches maturity. Most of us are willing to admit so much even to our own disadvantage, as well; and to become such a man as Aunt Betsey wants to make David into, and as Annie Strong seems now to be recommending, is to receive a fairy gift as precious to little boys as marrying Prince Charming used to be to little girls. To grow up to be such a man is indeed to become more than one's father, for as Aunt Betsey concludes, "That's what your father and mother might both have been, Heaven knows, and been the better for it." Surely every reader hopes along, both for his own sake and for David's, when David intimates that "I hoped I should be what she described" (p. 235), for it is deeply ingrained in our traditions, both the English and the American, that a young man cannot otherwise become the hero of his own life. This lesson is, in fact, older than *Tom Jones:* It is apparent in the life of Shakespeare's English hero-king, Henry V.

But, as we have seen, Annie Strong did not mean what Aunt Betsey had meant. To discipline the heart was not an English but a German lesson. It was not a preparation for heroic self-fulfillment but for selfless renunciation, not for manfully claiming one's proper woman at last but for loving her finally with so little "alloy of self" that one can "resign . . . [her] to a dearer protector . . . [and from a] removed place, [to] be a contented witness of . . . [her] joy" (p. 737). Thus when David comes at last to "discipline" his heart, he does not do so by heroically asserting and celebrating his manhood, as any male reader would like vicariously to do, but by the dutiful performance of an act of renunciation, which has been defined in this novel, in *The Battle of Life,* and elsewhere in Dickens, as a feminine quality. To love Agnes with a disciplined heart—and this is ironically the only way for David to win her—is to love her in the same way that women readers have been despising Agnes for loving *him*. It is to love her in the way that even Dora, one of the softest, least heroic characters in all literature, and the character in this novel with whom surely no reader, except perhaps G. K. Chesterton,[10] wants to identify, comes finally to love David when, on her deathbed, she resigns him to Agnes. Women readers do not like being told that they ought to love in this fashion; neither do men readers. And no reader is going to feel better about the situation after this reassurance that Dickens is not simply being sexist.

None of this is meant to suggest that Aunt Betsey is put-

---

10. Curiously the one thing Chesterton cannot forgive about Dora is her renunciation of David. He recognizes her as what I would call a Clown and what he calls a fool—"She represents the infinite and divine irrationality of the human heart"—but he cannot imagine "what possessed Dickens to make her such a dehumanized prig as to recommend her husband to marry another woman." *Charles Dickens,* pp. 267–68.

Daniel Maclise, "The Jeddler Sisters," 1846, from *The Battle of Life*. Courtesy of the University of California at Riverside Library.

ting David on the wrong track when she tries to toughen him up. Dickens is far from rejecting her lesson. David must indeed learn to be a man in the English sense of the term. If he stops at this goal, however, he will become a Steerforth or a Murdstone. He must also learn to be a woman, or to value feminine qualities in himself and in other men, like Traddles, whom Steerforth despises as "soft" (p. 363) and a "girl" (p. 86).[11] Dickens considered this to be so important a lesson that he undertook to learn it himself by writing half of his next novel from a woman's point of view.

David, the androgynous Principal Boy, is, moreover, both Harlequin and Columbine, and as Columbine he is surrounded, as we might expect, by a complete cast of pantomime characters. Aunt Betsey is still his Benevolent Agent, and Murdstone and Steerforth pursue him as Pantaloon and Dandy Lover. Dora is the self-sacrificing Dickensian Clown, which I will discuss in the next chapter. And just as Agnes is David's Columbine in his male identity, so is she the Harlequin of his female nature, incapable of acting or of speaking for herself, and dependent on the magical pious fraud of the Benevolent Agent to win her the lover she ardently desires. Thus David and Agnes each play the two dullest roles in the Christmas pantomime and are the most unattractively complex figures in the pantomime according to Dickens. They play the parts, moreover, that the hapless reader of Dickens, insidiously trapped into an identification with these characters, an identification amounting virtually to a self-indictment, persists testily in resenting. In a more healthful frame of mind, however, this uncomfortable identification might be perceived as a Dickensian "glaring instance" of the sort that

11. Merryn Williams, the author of *Women in the English Novel, 1800–1900*, argues that from *Dombey and Son* onward Dickens "thought that men would fail if they tried to live without 'female' values" (p. 78). In *"The Hero of My Life": Essays on Dickens* (Athens, Ohio, and London: Ohio University Press, 1981), Bert G. Hornback notes that "Steerforth is attractive to David in his strength and masculine forwardness . . . [but] David has to learn to appreciate the very different qualities that are Traddles'. He has to learn to respect Tommy's simple goodness and selfless ambition and . . . to appreciate Tommy's softness—and its femininity—as well" (p. 78).

brings Tattycoram of *Little Dorrit* and Bella Wilfer of *Our Mutual Friend* to their senses, allowing them to perceive the consequences of the lines of action they have taken and the logical conclusions of the worldviews they have adopted.

In the late novels, for reasons I shall discuss in the final chapter, such glaring instances, imaginative constructs of the pious frauds we discussed earlier, were supposed by Dickens to offer sufficient cause for a change of heart, both in the characters and in the uncomfortably identifying reader, as indeed they had in the five Christmas Books of the 1840s. Many readers and critics have remained unconvinced. But in the early novels, culminating with *David Copperfield*, the glaring instance was not required to perform such a heavy duty. It had merely to shake our complacency and make us want to change our lives. The conversion itself, a much more difficult task, was the province of the much-despised but truly heroic Clown. When James Fitzjames Stephen dismissed Dickens' intellect as feminine, this serious-minded critic also noted that it would be as foolish to argue with such a mind "as it would be to undertake a refutation of the jokes of the clown in a Christmas pantomime."[12] We shall see now why any attempted refutation of the Clown from the realist position that Stephen represented would be not only foolish but also utterly impossible.

12. James Fitzjames Stephen, "Mr. Dickens as a Politician," p. 8.

8

Clown: The Triumph of the Dickensian Absurd

The Clown is a delightful fellow to tickle our self-love with. He is very stupid, mischievous, gluttonous, and cowardly, none of which, of course, any of us are, especially the first; and as in these respects we feel a lofty advantage over him, so he occasionally aspires to our level by a sort of glimmering cunning and jocoseness, of which he thinks so prodigiously of himself as to give us a still more delightful notion of our superiority.

—Leigh Hunt

Grimaldi was a better clown. He made it a more intellectual performance.

—J. Wiston, Manager of Drury Lane
(early nineteenth century)

Micawber is not a man; Micawber is the superman. We can only walk round and round him wondering what we shall say. All the critics of Dickens, when all is said and done, have only walked round and round Micawber wondering what they should say. I am myself at this moment walking round and round Micawber wondering what I shall say. And I have not found it out yet.

—G. K. Chesterton

One of the major differences between melodrama and pantomime is that in the first the heroine, although of course she does not go to bed with anyone, has her most significant sexual relation with the villain, whom she despises, and in the second she has it with the Clown, whom she pities. The hero counts for little in either genre, and although he does end up marrying the girl, he has less energy, sexual or otherwise, than either the villain *or* the Clown, and the actor (or actress!) who plays him goes home with a much smaller paycheck than they do. The villain of melodrama is the starring role, as his counterpart in Gothic romance is frequently the title character, and after Grimaldi in England and Deburau in France, Clown was clearly the preeminent role in the pantomime.

In the French pantomime the love of the Clown Pierrot for Columbine is much more on the surface than it is in the English, but Pierrot was also an element in the development of the English Clown. Grimaldi's actor father, who had played first on the Continent, was known on the English stage as "the rough and tumble pierrot."[1] In *Harlequin and Cinderella* (1820) Joey himself created the part of the servant, Pedro, who is hopelessly in love with the heroine. This character, now called Buttons, is still played by the leading male actor in modern English productions of *Cinderella*. Moreover, in the harlequinade chase after the lovers the essential behavior of the English and French clowns was similar. There is sometimes less pathos and tension in those English pantos where Clown does not love Columbine but only rebels against Pantaloon and respectability, but S. R. Littlewood's account of the French pantomime in *The Story of Pierrot* serves also as an apt description of what usually happened on the English pantomime stage:

> At last . . . Harlequin did absolutely run off with Columbine. Then Pierrot wakes up to join in the pursuit with his old master, Pantaloon, and all the rest of them. It was always Pierrot who knew where the lovers were; but as often as not he helped them to escape, and then went blundering on with the others again.[2]

Clown as Buttons or Pedro or Pierrot appears in a number of Dickens' novels. One of the earliest of these appearances is

---

1. Findlater, *Joe Grimaldi: His Life and Theatre*, p. 36.
2. S. R. Littlewood, *The Story of Pierrot*, (London: Herbert and Daniel, 1911), pp. 33–34.

as Smike, the crippled outcast, whose hopeless love for Kate Nickleby is obviously influenced, although perhaps indirectly, by Deburau's creation. The following wordless scene, which describes Smike after he has discovered that Kate and Frank Cheeryble love one another, was being mimed pretty regularly during the 1830s by the sad clown in the French pantomime:

> Who was that who, in the silence of his own chamber, sunk upon his knees to pray as his first friend had taught him, and folding his hands and stretching them wildly in the air, fell upon his face in a passion of bitter grief? (Chap. 43, p. 566)

Mr. Toots of *Dombey and Son* is another such lover. Others in this line include Tom Pinch of *Martin Chuzzlewit*, Mr. Guppy of *Bleak House*, John Chivery of *Little Dorrit*, and, with the smile wiped entirely off our faces, Sydney Carton of *A Tale of Two Cities*. When, as we have heard Paul Schlicke explain,[3] Kit Nubbles was introduced as a clown in the early chapters of *Old Curiosity Shop*, he was probably intended for a Pierrot, for it is impossible to suppose he was ever intended to win the ethereal Nell. The chief facts about each of these characters are that they love the heroine, that they are somehow defective, and, at least after Smike, that they render significant assistance to the heroine, assistance that usually involves some sort of self-sacrifice. Toots' action of finding Susan Nipper may be "of no consequence," as he would say, but it is at least disinterested, energetic, and effective, and he is one of the first characters in Dickens who has to learn the difficult, in his case the excruciatingly painful business of disciplining his heart, of being happy for Florence as she marries Walter. The difference between the clown character's capacity for action and that of the virtually paralyzed hero, is clearest in the comparison between Sydney Carton and Charles Darnay, but Guppy and Chivery also rise far above themselves to serve the ladies whom they also can never win. Even before Mr.

3. See chap. 1, p. 18.

Toots, Tom Pinch sacrifices Pecksniff for Mary's sake, although he recognizes with considerable maturity that his hope of winning her was only "a dream . . . something that might possibly have happened under very different circumstances, but which can never be" (chap. 50, p. 763).

Other Dickensian Clowns are less obviously attached to heroines. Dick Swiveller, for instance, gives up his unworthy ambition to marry Nell, but that he recognizes the woman he ultimately does marry as the heroine's double is apparent from his "remark at divers subsequent periods that there had been a young lady saving up for him after all" (Chapter the Last, p. 551). Still others, Newman Noggs, for instance, never aspire romantically, and some, like Sissy Jupe and Jenny Wren, who also serve the heroines at crucial moments, are not even of the right gender to marry the heroine. What they all have in common, once again, are their somehow defective natures and their capacities, not only to act, but to act as rescuers. Sissy, the circus child who is brought into the Utilitarian Gradgrind household to serve only as a negative example, saves the sensibly educated Louisa when her shaken father fails to do so, and Noggs, whom Ralph Nickleby dismisses as "a fellow . . . who would sell his soul (if he had one) for drink, and whose every word is a lie" (chap. 59, p. 773), is the man who foils Ralph's plot to defraud Madeline. Q. D. Leavis, like many readers before and after her, believes that Micawber is "*improbably* made the agent of Heep's downfall,"[4] and Heep is himself surprised, for he calls Micawber "a dissipated fellow, as all the world knows. . . . the very scum of society" (pp. 639–40). In the same novel Dora Spenlow Copperfield, who disciplines her own heart just before she dies and surprisingly serves as an example for David in his feminine identity, is despised by nearly everyone. Shaw says of her:

> There is a remarkable combination of tenderness and ruthlessness in the picture of Dora. She is made to appear utterly worthless and useless, so incorrigibly silly and spoiled, that

---

4. Q. D. Leavis, *Dickens the Novelist*, p. 87; emphasis added.

Kant himself would have denied her the right of an individual to be considered as an end rather than as a means, and would have admitted that her death was an inevitable consequence of the absence of any moral reason why she should live.[5]

Yet Dickens from quite early in his career had been using these seemingly worthless and morally inconsequential characters as his only heroic actors. Lord Frederick Verisopht, who loses his life defending Kate Nickleby's honor, is the first in a line of Dickens' characters which was to lead ultimately to Sydney Carton of *A Tale of Two Cities*.[6] Lord Frederick is also a variety of Clown. As with Dora, no reader, and certainly no character in the novel, takes him seriously until the time for his heroic, self-sacrificing action arrives.

The other Clowns in *David Copperfield* are similarly despised, and none seems to be a probable rescuer. Mr. Dick is a good example. Everyone in the novel except Aunt Betsey, the Benevolent Spirit who can see through appearances, regards him with either contempt or condescension. That he seems to be the least consequential character in the novel, however, is precisely what gives him the power to act effectively. He can save Annie Strong's marriage because, as he says,

> "A poor fellow with a craze . . . a simpleton, a weak-minded person—present company, you know—. . . may do what wonderful people may not do. I'll bring them together, boy. I'll try. They'll not blame *me*. They'll not object to *me*. They'll not mind what *I* do, if it's wrong. I'm only Mr. Dick. And who minds Dick? Dick's nobody! Whoo!" He blew a slight contemptuous breath, as if he blew himself away. (P. 558)

Mr. Dick is an amusing eccentric, but it is not strictly necessary in Dickens for these seemingly worthless rescuers, these pantomime Clowns, to be comic. A very unfunny character plays the significant role in a pantomime plot told in chapter sixty of *Nicholas Nickleby*, the briefly sketched history of Smike's unfortunate mother. In this story of an unhappy, se-

---

5. *Shaw on Dickens*, pp. 17–18.
6. See Pratt, "Carlyle and Dickens."

cret marriage followed by a tragic elopement Ralph Nickleby, the mercenary husband, is the unsuitable lover. Meanwhile the woman's guardian, her "rough, fox-hunting, hard drinking" brother, is Pantaloon, and Harlequin is the ineffectual "younger man" with whom the doomed Columbine makes her desperate and futile escape. The one character who is able to act effectively is Brooker, the clerk who served Ralph Nickleby before Newman Noggs. This humorless character, who always enters the action like Nemesis in the melodrama, might seem, in spite of his capacity for action, to have little in common with the harlequinade Clown, and indeed he does not act for any benevolent purpose, but it is perhaps worth mentioning that Dickens found his name in the life story of Grimaldi, which he was editing at the time he was writing *Nicholas Nickleby*. Rebecca Brooker was the famous Clown's unwed mother.

The Nemesis character in *David Copperfield*, the unfunny Clown who appears mysteriously throughout the novel like a dark shadow, is the prostitute Martha, Emily's unlikely rescuer, who occupies the very lowest station. "A poor wurem," as Ham Peggotty describes her, "trod under foot by all the town. Up street and down street. The mowld o' the churchyard don't hold any that the folk shrink away from, more" (p. 287). Later on Mr. Peggotty recounts Martha's rescue of Emily in language that relates the situation to Emily's death-avoiding motive for trying to become a lady and at the same time signifies the heroic dimensions of Martha's accomplishment:

> She says to her, "Rise up from worse than death, and come with me!" Them belonging to the house would have stopped her, but they might as soon have stopped the sea. "Stand away from me," she says, "I am a ghost that calls her from beside her open grave!" (P. 623)

To rescue from death—this is indeed the function of the Dickensian Clown from Swiveller to Carton, as it was the false promise of the villainous Dandy Lover. It is an especially important function in *David Copperfield*, in which, as we have seen, both the hero and his first love are obsessed with the fear of death. As Mr. Peggotty said, Martha Endell is more powerful than the sea, which is soon to kill Ham and Steerforth, but *her* strength is to rescue. To save from death was also the function of Grimaldi's pantomime Clown, as Jackson Cope describes him:

> Joey became the English Clown . . . by crossing the subterranean subversiveness of the older Arlecchino with the manner and stupid shrewdness of the English country fellow, and by setting the whole in an England which gave it a local habitation and "verisimilitude" against which the extravagant triumph of life over death, the daemonic over the daily, could be played out.[7]

Except for poor, pale Dora none of the Clowns of *David Copperfield* can be regarded as a Pierrot figure. Ham Peggotty, who tries literally to rescue his rival Steerforth, is the closest to the type of this sad clown, faithful though rejected. "He follers her [Emily] about," Mr. Peggotty says, "he makes hisself a sort o' sarvant to her" (p. 267). As a very young boy, David is also a comic lover to Emily, threatening to kill himself with a sword if she does not confess that she adores him (p. 32), and Martha speaks of Emily in terms appropriate to the courtly and religious love tradition, of which Pierrot is perhaps a late reflection: "When I lost everything that makes life dear, the worst of all my thoughts was that I was parted for ever from her" (p. 582).

When we first see Martha and Emily together, Martha is looking up to a window where Emily holds a light. It is a reverential scene, "solemn," as Ham Peggotty describes it. "Em'ly, Em'ly, for Christ's sake have a woman's heart towards me" (p. 287). This image of the despised figure gazing upward as at a star at the heroine he or she will rescue binds together the Clown-lovers of *David Copperfield*. Doctor Strong's

---

7. Jackson Cope, *Dramaturgy and the Daemonic: Studies in Antigeneric Theatre from Ruzante to Grimaldi* (Baltimore: Johns Hopkins University Press, 1984), p. 13.

" 'beautiful wife is a star,' said Mr. Dick. 'A shining star. I have seen her shine'" (p. 557). And " 'Miss Wickfield,' said Mr. Micawber, now turning red, 'is, as she always always is, a pattern and a bright example. My dear Copperfield, she is the only starry spot in a miserable existence'" (p. 603). Like Dora, these worshipful, degenerate lovers provide examples for David, who, in his first clownish dissipation, mistakenly acknowledged Steerforth as "theguidingstarofmyexist ence" (p. 308), and, still caught up in his first infatuation with the genteel proctor's daughter, spoke of "the star of Dora" shining brightly and purely "high above the world" (p. 404). Later, however, he sees Agnes Wickfield, "ever a star above me . . . brighter and higher" (p. 720), and he finally perceives her face "shining on me like a Heavenly light by which I see all other objects" (p. 751).

Micawber, who points out this true celestial light most directly for David, is the ultimate Clown of *David Copperfield* and indeed of all Dickens' novels. His relation to the lovers is prototypical and so also is his association with the villain. Let me explain. Perhaps the most interesting of the repeated patterns since the Dickens pantomime began in earnest with *Nicholas Nickleby* has been the temporary bondage, as in the pantomime itself, of the Clown to the evil or repressive forces of the novel. Both Newman Noggs and Brooker are the despised wage slaves of Ralph Nickleby, whom they ultimately overturn, and, until his surprising rebellion, Lord Frederick Verisopht appears to be entirely under the spell of Sir Mulberry Hawk. In *The Old Curiosity Shop* Dick Swiveller goes to work for the Quilp faction and becomes an unwitting tool in the plot against Kit Nubbles. Barnaby Rudge waves a banner in the No Popery Riots. "If ever man believed with his whole heart and soul that he was engaged in a just cause, and that he was bound to stand by his leader to the last, poor Barnaby believed it of himself and Lord George Gordon" (chap. 49, p. 378). In *Martin Chuzzlewit* Tom Pinch believes in Pecksniff, almost as an article of faith, and in the novels after *David Copperfield* Mr. Guppy and Sydney Carton are minions of the law and of the deadly Old Testament values that it does or sometimes does not dispense. John Chivery of *Little Dorrit* is the son of the Lock at the Marshalsea. Micawber, of course, appears for a time to have sold his soul to Uriah Heep.

This relationship mirrors the situation in the harlequinade chase, where Clown is the servant of Pantaloon, and we shall have to look at the pantomime again when we come shortly to discuss the meaning behind the slave rebellions of Micawber and the others. We must first, however, concern ourselves with the significance in Dickens of the relationship itself. The villain, who promises life but delivers death, is, as we have seen, the false hero in the Dickens pantomime. In a world where Harlequin is too burdened with guilt to act and where Columbine needs to be rescued, only the villain, the worst of the dramatis personae, seems to have what Yeats would later call the "passionate intensity" necessary for action. David and Emily, as we have seen, look to Steerforth to save them from death, and while no character in the novel is tempted to surrender himself or herself to Uriah, in fact Heep's combination of humility and self-help had become a more popular Victorian, daydream road to salvation than marriage to a gentleman. We have also seen that both these roads, the ways of self-assertion, lead toward death rather than away from it.

At the moment when the villain employs the Clown, he seems to be making an odd choice: He does not appear to have gained a useful servant, and he does not pretend to value his acquisition. Nor, at least at a conscious or rational level, is the reader very much concerned. The Clown seems more of a liability than an asset to the villain. When David hears that Micawber has found employment with Heep, he restrains his enthusiasm somewhat because he is afraid Uriah will find out about his shameful and humiliating episode at Murdstone and Grinby. But this is hardly a concern for the reader, who is busy at the moment either forgiving David or condemning both him and Dickens for this piece of snobbish sensitivity. As things turn out, moreover, the villain has made a serious mistake, for the despised servant always proves to be his undoing. Does the villain sense that this representative of the seemingly least powerful, whom he publicly despises, is the only force capable of standing against him? Is the villain trying subconsciously to co-opt this force, as when James Carker, gaining control over Rob the Grinder, tries to harness the Toodles' power of the railroad that is destined ultimately to grind up his life? In any event, it is likely that the reader in a subrational or superrational way recognizes the potential of the Clown's power, and thus when Micawber enters Heep's employ and goes deeply into his debt, the villain seems to have expanded his empire of darkness so that it threatens to cover the entire created world of the novel. At least at the comic level, which is always the essential level in Dickens, the dark night of the soul, the pantomimic Dark Scene, occurs in *David Copperfield* when Mrs. Micawber reports the assertion of her husband "(formerly so domesticated)" that "he has sold himself to the D," and when she writes "in extreme distress" that "he presented an oyster-knife at the twins" (pp. 600–601).

In the pantomime, the following situation is the given: Clown seems to be little better than a slave to Pantaloon and is expected, usually, to assist in the plot against Harlequin and Columbine. Clown's very nature, however, rebels. Richard Findlater called Grimaldi's Clown "a Cockney incarnation of the saturnalian spirit; a beloved criminal, free from guilt, shame, compunction, or reverence for age, class or property." Elsewhere Findlater wrote that Joey "persecuted Pantaloon, lusted after Columbine, guzzled on a grand scale, stole and was robbed, cheated and was gulled, beat people up, pushed them over, tripped them up, and was himself mercilessly thrashed, kicked and cudgelled."[8] David Mayer, the best historian of Regency pantomime, writes even more exuberantly of this character:

> If Clown encountered another's property he would break it if fragile, wear it if portable, paint it or deface it if immovable. If there was a woman, old or young, he would make advances; if there was food he would eat it gluttonously; if the food were

---

8. Richard Findlater, *Joe Grimaldi: His Life and Theatre*, p. 160, and "Introduction," *Memoirs of Joseph Grimaldi*, ed. Charles Dickens, p. 21.

Clown, from a Juvenile Drama Sheet, circa 1830.

someone else's he would first steal it. The law held terror for him only when he was in danger of being caught. He was a happy criminal, who knew neither shame nor guilt nor repentance. He was a mimic, a coward; a lazy rascal, an energetic imposter.[9]

Grimaldi's Clown did nominally join the harlequinade chase and sometimes seemed even to lead it. But his was not the sort of nature finally to support self-righteous authority. He had, Mayer writes,

> a buoyancy, a barely suppressed impudence and irreverence that encouraged pantomime audiences to share vicariously, and willingly condone his seeming impatience with manners, his mocking of class distinctions, his disregard for property, and his absolute disrespect for authority. If Clown had fixed traits, they were all ones that mocked conventions and exposed social habits pretending to morality and self-conscious graciousness. He rebelled against stuffiness and tradition. . . . He humiliated the mighty, the cruel, the pretentious and the overbearing.[10]

Such a character could not long remain Pantaloon's ally, however inept, in the battle against the young people. In fact he is the natural enemy of both Pantaloon and Dandy Lover, who represent the establishment, and while Clown may be forced for a while to gain his living as Pantaloon's servant, he can be expected to undermine and betray his master in every imaginable way. While pretending to help the old man, as A. E. Wilson explains, he "constantly gets into scrapes and puts him on the wrong scent."[11] He never becomes the outright champion of the lovers, as the bluff and hearty Comic Man in melodrama does, for, as we have seen, pantomime is a more basically anarchical form than melodrama. Michael Booth has made the distinction between the two forms in a

---

9. David Mayer, *Harlequin in His Element* (Cambridge, Mass.: Harvard University Press, 1969), pp. 44–47.
10. Ibid.
11. A. E. Wilson, *King Panto: The Story of Pantomime* (New York: E. P. Dutton, 1935), p. 41.

way that may help to clarify the difference between these two men of action:

> The harlequinade was, like melodrama, psychologically escapist, offering audiences a release for sadistic impulses toward cheating, tricking, larceny, cruelty, wanton destruction, violence, and rebellion. Melodrama, however, idealized morality, revered the aged parent, rewarded virtue and punished vice; pantomime satisfied different desires and did the exact opposite. The same audiences enjoyed both genres, and both found common ground in a general hostility toward constituted and inherited authority. In melodrama this was largely a matter of class conflict, but in pantomime the same hostility manifested itself in vicious treatment of an oppressive father-figure, Pantaloon and his watchman or policeman surrogate.[12]

---

12. Booth, "Introduction," *English Plays of the Nineteenth Century*, 5: 5–6. The anarchical exuberance of the clown is well illustrated by a routine called "Nursing the Baby," which is quoted here from a harlequinade scenario:

> Toss the baby to Pantaloon, crying "Catchee, catchee!" Snatch it away from him, and hit him with it over the shins, knocking him down. Squat upon the ground with the baby in your lap and begin feeding it out of a large pan with a great dripping ladle. Ram the ladle into the mouth of the baby, then scrape the lips with the edge of it, then lick them clean. Now wash the baby by putting it in a tub, pouring the water on it from the kettle, and swabbing its face with a mop. Comb its hair with a rake; then put the baby into a mangle and roll it out flat. Set the baby in the cradle and tread it well down. Make the baby cry; then take it out of the bed to quiet it, and give it to Pantaloon to hold whilst you administer poppy syrup. Smear the syrup over its face. Take it away again, catch hold of its ankles, and swinging it around your head by its legs, thrash the Pantaloon off the stage with the baby, and throw it after him.

This routine, quoted from a publication of the 1880s, James Johnson, *Johnson's Account of Pantomime* (London: H. S. Phillips, 1884), may have been more destructive than the Clown of Dickens' imagination but not markedly so. Here, for instance, is Gautier's description of the great mid-century English Clown, Richard Flexmore, as he appeared in *Harlequin et Hudibras* in 1853:

> He is a strapping athletic fellow, with prominent pectorals and knotty biceps, stuffed full of bloody roastbeef, glutted with whiskey and gin, stoked with ginger, cayenne pepper, and Indian spices. Two spots of blood mottle his powdered cheeks; red gashes lengthen his mouth to a maw and give him an air of cannibalistic voraciousness: you would think he was a man-eater who had just bitten into a morsel of human flesh. From his greedy ravenousness to the epicurism of the French

The pantomime Clown is too anarchical a figure to support even an as yet uncorrupted establishment-in-the-bud, such as the victorious Harlequin and Columbine represent, but his wild, destructive, out-of-control actions serve, nevertheless, to aid them against the patriarchy.

Obviously most of Dickens' clowns, who had to make their way as at least somewhat believable characters in supposedly mimetic works of Victorian fiction, pale in comparison with this awesome figure. As we have seen, Newman Noggs looks and acts like the Clown of pantomime. He also has a penchant for making pantomimic gestures, especially hostile gestures directed at Ralph Nickleby, his Pantaloon enemy and master. These comical mime actions are significant, for Newman and the other characters in *Nicholas Nickleby* whom I have designated as clowns, Brooker and Lord Frederick, are worthy of the title largely because they share an apparently impotent hostility. In time they all show their hidden strength, but none of them, not even Noggs, has anything like the comic energy of the pantomime Clown, or his power to destroy the hierarchy or to renew the world. This was still to come in Dickens.

Another Dickensian degenerate, Dick Swiveller, approximates more closely the chaotic disorder of the pantomime

---

Pierrot there is all the distance that separates the glutton from the gourmand. He is like the ostrich: he swallows the oyster and the shell, the wine and the bottle, the joint and the skewer: he would gladly eat the table, and would digest it with as little trouble. He had truculent and formidable accesses of gayety, like an ogre in fine spirits; for every blow of the slapstick he receives, he sends back a punch that would kill a bull or a boxer. If he gives you a handshake, he dislocates your wrist and tears off your shoulder; his only natal air is fighting and mischief; he smashes the decorations, beats the supernumeraries half to death, and amuses himself in the action like a bull in a china shop. The other characters—Harlequin, Hudibras, Colombine—provoke him only with a respectful terror.

Gautier's review was published in *La Presse*, 8 August 1853, and was translated by Robert Storey and printed in his book, *Pierrots on the Stage of Desire: Nineteenth Century French Literary Artists and the Comic Pantomime* (Princeton: Princeton University Press, 1985), p. 32.

Clown's comedy. Paul Schlicke has shown how Swiveller's Grimaldian "determination to welcome every experience" permits him to emerge "in a world of fear and destruction as a positive force for life."[13] His superhuman capacity for heroic action can be appreciated at an even higher level, as Steven Marcus asserts when he writes that in rescuing the Marchioness, "Swiveller has descended into the Kingdom of Death, the true *mise en scène* of the novel, and reclaimed someone from it. He has done nothing less than create another person; he has given her an identity, brought her up out of darkness into life."[14] This passage serves to describe the accomplishments of the unfunny Clown Martha in *David Copperfield* and of the tragic resurrectionist Sydney Carton in *A Tale of Two Cities*.

But Dickens' ultimate Clown, Wilkins Micawber, eclipsed even Grimaldi's comic creation and served as a bridge between Grimaldi's Clown and such twentieth-century clowns as W. C. Fields and Charlie Chaplin. James R. Kincaid has written that Micawber and his wife "climax a great line of Dickens's comic characters and carry on the role of Sam Weller as tutor and seer, Dick Swiveller as parodist, Sairey Gamp as imaginative creator."[15]

In *The English Comic Character* J. B. Priestley sees Micawber as, "with the one exception of Falstaff . . . the greatest comic figure in the whole range of English literature, a literature supremely rich in such characters."[16] The implied comparison between Micawber and Falstaff is both apt and common.[17] Chesterton must have been thinking of it when he expressed unhappiness at what he took to be David's and Dickens' ban-

---

13. Schlicke, *Dickens and Popular Entertainment*, p. 135.
14. Steven Marcus, *Dickens from Pickwick to Dombey* (London: Chatto and Windus, 1965), p. 167.
15. Kincaid, *Dickens and the Rhetoric of Laughter*, p. 178.
16. J. B. Priestley, *The English Comic Character* (New York: Phaeton Press, 1972), p. 213.
17. See, for instance, Sir John Shuckburgh's "Wilkins Micawber," *Dickensian* 45 (1949): 125–28.

Hablot Browne, "Mr. Swiveller Playing the Flute," 1840, from *The Old Curiosity Shop*. Courtesy of the University of California at Riverside Library.

ishing Micawber to Australia, and it is true that Dickens had been working toward such a rival creation since he first thought of Mr. Pickwick's belly. Several months before he began writing *David Copperfield*, Dickens played the part of Justice Shallow opposite his friend Mark Lemon, the editor of *Punch* and the author of successful pantomimes, who played Falstaff in Dickens' own production of *The Merry Wives of Windsor*. "My address," said Mr. Micawber, "is Windsor Terrace, City Road" (p. 134). In this fashion, after acknowledging his name with an "Ahem!" he introduces himself to David and to the world.

What Falstaff and Micawber have in common includes the pretension to gentility, and they both share with Grimaldi's Clown a questionable moral character,[18] an improvident life style, and an immense appetite, not only for life, but quite literally for food and drink. Bernard Schilling writes of Micawber:

> Apart from a number of suppers, breakfasts, and teas of unspecified ingredients, we sit down with the Micawbers at various times to veal cutlet, cheese, loin of mutton, lamb's fry, shrimps, loin of pork, apple sauce, pudding, kidney pie, ale, brandy and water, flip, breaded lamb chops, fish, roast loin of veal, red sausage meat, partridge, wine, leg of mutton and gravy, pigeon pie, and—every time there is the least excuse for it—punch, veritable lakes of punch.[19]

"Above all," writes William Oddie, "the picture that remains is of Mr. Micawber eating and, especially, drinking or preparing for drinking, the image of him seen through a cloud of rising steam."[20]

Another related comic character whom Micawber seems intended to recall is the pantomime favorite, Humpty Dumpty.

---

18. Orwell says that David is "ultimately bound to see Mr. Micawber for what he is, a cadging scoundrel." "Charles Dickens," in *Dickens, Dali and Others*, p. 67.
19. Bernard Schilling, *The Comic Spirit: Boccaccio to Thomas Mann* (Detroit: Wayne State University Press, 1965), p. 106.
20. William Oddie, "Mr. Micawber and the Redefinition of Experience," *Dickensian* 63 (1967): 106.

Thus Micawber is first described as "a stoutish, middle-aged person, in a brown surtout and black tights and shoes, with no more hair upon his head (which was a large one, and very shining) than there is upon an egg, and with a very extensive face, which he turned full upon me. His clothes were shabby, but he had an imposing shirt-collar on" (p. 134). Humpty Dumpty falls down in the pantomime as in the nursery rhyme, but in the pantomime this is by no means the end of him. He is an egg, after all, and when his shell breaks, a new, still comic, but surprisingly heroic character emerges, one capable of striking a blow on behalf of Harlequin or the Principal Boy.[21]

This regenerative quality also relates Micawber and Falstaff, both of whom are continually rebounding from defeat and humiliation and apparently returning symbolically from the dead, either from the sword of the Douglas or the fell power of Heep. And, as we have seen, this ability to die and yet somehow remain alive was for Dickens the chief attraction of the "jocund world of pantomime," where "there is no affliction or calamity that leaves the least impression."[22]

For Micawber, the ability to escape consequences springs from the power of language, which he uses as grandly and thriftlessly as he uses food or drink or money. Clown is the only speaking and singing part in the otherwise wordless harlequinade, and Dickens' clowns, from Dick Swiveller onward, are masters of speech. Michael Edwards writes of Mrs. Gamp, whom he sees as a development from the Shakespearean clown, as one who makes "a fresh language-world for us, imaginatively exhilarating and humanely warm as a triumph of nonsense over sense, . . . fool's babble [that] hangs between an unprecedented order and chaos, between Pentecostal speech and a clownish gibber."[23] The magic of speech, according to Schilling, gives Micawber his principal power:

---

21. Births from giant eggs are common even in pantomimes that do not involve Humpty Dumpty.
22. Dickens, "A Curious Dance Round a Curious Tree," p. 385.
23. Michael Edwards, *Towards a Christian Poetics* (London: Macmillan, 1984), p. 71.

Human greatness is not to be defeated. Soaring above all misery on the wings of metaphor, this tremendous fool can welcome the very specters that long have menaced him and his family. When "mutual confidence" has been restored between himself and his wife, Micawber cries out an ecstatic greeting to the worst that life can array against him.

"Now welcome poverty!" cried Mr. Micawber, shedding tears. "Welcome misery, welcome houselessness, welcome hunger, rags, tempest, and beggary! Mutual confidence will sustain us to the end!"

The problems of life are met with the same abstractions as always, and the specters are routed in their own terms. The fact is defeated by the word, the menace is banished by the metaphor, and poverty becomes only a word or a notion, not an affair of food and clothing. So the great optimist cries defiance to this "variety of bleak prospects" and calls upon his wife and family to come forth and sing a chorus.[24]

Such a tribute gives a fair notion of Micawber's power, but it is an example finally of a critic walking round and round Micawber, as Chesterton justly says we all are, wondering what in the world he should say. It fails to get at Micawber's essence, I believe, because it mistakes his function in the plot of *David Copperfield*. Clown is not Harlequin, and his purpose in the story is not to save himself. Even Micawber recognizes, when he believes he is acting to explode himself along with Heep, that the Clown must die. The happy ending that Dickens imagined for Micawber, and which so many readers have objected to either because they think the man could not succeed under any circumstances or because they want him to succeed or continue failing in England rather than abroad, is not so much a safe harbor for him as it is a possibility for us. Influenced by Carlyle and deeply involved in his Urania Cottage scheme, Dickens was trying to create Australia as a real place in the minds of trapped English men and women. Thus Australia does not regenerate Micawber so much as Micawber

---

24. Schilling, *Comic Spirit*, pp. 113–14. Similarly, J. Hillis Miller sees Micawber's "perpetual transcendence of spirit over concrete reality" as a "transcendence through language" (*Charles Dickens: The World of His Novels*, p. 151).

generates Australia, and if, as Thackeray wrote, there was a run on turkeys after the publication of *A Christmas Carol*,[25] then I suspect the booking offices for the Australia lines must have been busy after the final number of *David Copperfield*. The purpose of the Clown, as Dickens was to show unequivocally in *A Tale of Two Cities*, is to save the lovers and, more importantly still, to redeem the readers.

The circumambulating critic who has found the most interesting things to say about Micawber is James R. Kincaid, who sees him as "the architect and most enthusiastic builder" of a "subversive structure . . . the comic world of the imagination," which Dickens tried in all of his earlier novels to set against "the threatening and hostile world of practical or commercial 'reality.'"[26] Clown is, indeed, subversive. Not only Bakhtin but all the commentators on pantomime would agree that this is what Clown is all about, and Micawber is, among other things, Dickens' way of striking at the Malthusian principles which were, so he fervently believed, crippling his country and his century. As Raymond Chapman says in *The Victorian Debate*, Micawber, "feckless and unsystematic, cocks a snook at these principles and emerges triumphant."[27] And Humphry House has written, "He seems a direct and unqualified affront to the whole little prudent philosophy."[28] Even more relevantly to the problems of *David*

---

25. Thackeray wrote, "A Scotch philosopher, who nationally does not keep Christmas Day, on reading the book, sent out for a turkey, and asked two friends to dine—this is a fact! Many men were known to sit down after perusing it, and write off letters to their friends, and not about business, but out of their fulness of heart, and to wish old acquaintances a happy Christmas." "A Box of Novels," *Frasers Magazine* 29 (February 1844). Reprinted in *Charles Dickens: A Critical Anthology*, ed. Stephen Wall (Harmondsworth: Penguin, 1970), p. 65.

26. Kincaid, *Dickens and the Rhetoric of Laughter*, p. 165.

27. Raymond Chapman, *The Victorian Debate* (London: Weidenfield and Nicolson, 1968), p. 113.

28. Humphry House, *The Dickens World* (London, New York, Toronto: Oxford University Press, 1942), p. 84. House also writes:

> If we judge Mr. Micawber by his behaviour throughout the greater part of *David Copperfield*, there could be no more wanton violator of the rules of Malthus and Smiles. He is the personification of unthrift; he

Copperfield, Micawber serves to liberate everyone from the paralysis imposed by the hierarchical society of England.[29] He also rescues us from this society's suicidal pretension to gentility, for which, as Harvey Peter Sucksmith notes, "he provides a burlesque."[30]

According to House, "The moral of Micawber . . . is that even in a man as fantastically improvident and as gay about it as he, there is a secret possibility of success."

> Micawber got the better of the prudent philosophers both on the swings and on the roundabouts. For sixty-two chapters he was saying in the very best Dickens manner, 'See how wonderful and lovable a thoroughly unthrifty and imprudent man can be,' and in the sixty-third he turned round and showed that even he could do well enough for himself when the right thing turned up.[31]

This is an excessively optimistic reading of the conclusion and must be balanced against Kincaid's belief that when "Micawber moves to Australia, the impossibility of a comic society must finally, and sadly, be admitted."[32] Kincaid is right, of course, and the note of sadness that so many readers of *David Copperfield* have heard cannot be denied, nor can it be disconnected, as Chesterton emphasized, from the banishment of plump Micawber. But surely this regret is sentimental wishful thinking. No one can seriously believe that Micawber's comic world ever had a chance of becoming a permanent establishment any more than the green world in *As You Like It*

---

goes on begetting children for whom he cannot provide; he refuses to toe the misery-line; he accepts charitable loans that he cannot possibly hope to repay; he finally has to emigrate on somebody else's money; yet Dickens loves him beyond words. (P. 84)

29. In "The Englishness of Dickens," *Etudes Anglais* 23 (1970), E.W.F. Tomlin writes that without this hierarchy "it would have been difficult to invent Micawber" (p. 118).

30. Harvey Peter Sucksmith, *The Narrative Art of Charles Dickens: The Rhetoric of Sympathy and Irony in His Novels* (Oxford: Oxford University Press, 1970), p. 190.

31. House, *The Dickens World,* p. 85.

32. Kincaid, *Dickens and the Rhetoric of Laughter,* p. 167.

could have forever remained Duke Senior's court or the Island a permanent home for Prospero. That was never its function anyway. The Clown and his carnival destroy establishments, and we had better use the liberation his gift affords to repair ourselves than to waste it in dreaming of Christmases all year round, although, admittedly, it is Dickens who has craftily encouraged this idle wish.

Kincaid and I disagree most sharply when he argues that Micawber is subversive to the philosophy of the disciplined heart. If to discipline one's heart means no more than to become what Aunt Betsey called a self-respecting English gentleman, then Kincaid would be right in calling it "a terribly reductive formula for a humane and responsive existence . . . priggish, escapist, ugly, and narrow . . . [a formula that] denies the values that count—those of Dora, the Micawbers, and Mr. Dick" (p. 163). But, as we have seen, this is not what is meant by disciplining one's heart. When David achieves a disciplined heart at last, he has not adopted the humorless and hardheaded values of Murdstone or the self-assertiveness of Uriah Heep; he has come at last to love Agnes in the pliable way that allows of no hardening alloy of self, in the manner of the matured Dora, who even wishes herself dead so that David can find fulfillment with Agnes, and of the other Clowns, who act selflessly to serve the lady, "the only starry spot in an otherwise miserable existence."

Coming as it does before the deaths of Dora and Steerforth, the sentimental and sensational climaxes of the novel, Micawber's explosion of Heep, comical and at the same time self-sacrificing, liberates David to understand the ordeals he is to pass through. If it makes Micawber's Australian fortune for him, that is irrelevant. Its purpose is to free the novel from the empire of death, as instituted in the self-help philosophy of Heep, the sexton's son. It fulfills this function for David by somehow permitting him to face the very fact of death, which he has been avoiding from the beginning of the novel.

David Copperfield contains more deaths of individualized characters than any Dickens novel except *Bleak House*. David's father died before he was born, and in the course of his narrated life all of his relatives die except Aunt Betsey. Up to the crucial point in the novel where Micawber exposes Heep, David has lost his mother, his father-in-law, his infant brother, and his first child. Garrett Stewart has noted that *David Copperfield* is the only work "before *Malone Dies* that has invented a new word for death, 'drowndead.'"[33] And yet, despite this emphasis and this quantity of deaths, and despite the fact that Dickens, who had just completed *Dombey and Son*, was justly famous for his death scenes, the only deathbed at which David Copperfield has himself been present was that of Barkis. The exception is as notable as the suppression. The miser is traditionally understood as one who seeks to avoid death,[34] and Barkis's unwillingness in this regard is made clear in *his* significant omission of the word *death* in a well-known folk saying:

> "It was as true," said Mr. Barkis, "as turnips is. It was as true," said Mr. Barkis, nodding his nightcap, which was his only means of emphasis, "as taxes is. And nothing's truer than them." (P. 263)

David takes little part in the exposure of Heep's villainy, although Uriah keeps looking at him as if he, rather than Traddles, Mr. Dick, and Micawber, were the chief actor. This incapacity for action is, as noted, typical of a Harlequin. For a long time David does not even speak. " 'Has that Copperfield no tongue?' muttered Uriah" (p. 649). But the effect of the scene is that when David finally does find his tongue, at last, it is to complete the suppressed part of Barkis's analogy: "There never were greed and cunning in the world yet," David says, "that did not do too much, and over-reach themselves. It is as certain as death" (p. 650). David, the novelist ghost-seer of memory and imagination, who began the novel by insisting that although born with the privilege "to see ghosts and spirits" (p. 1), he has never seen any, is, with Micawber's help, growing out of his terror.

The word precedes the deed, however, for in the next

---

33. Stewart, *Death Sentences*, p. 73.
34. See George Anastaplo, *The Artist as Thinker: From Shakespeare to Joyce* (Chicago: Swallow Press, 1984), p. 127.

chapter David is still not free of his paralysis. He tells us that he "cannot master" the thought of Dora's death (p. 656), and, when her death comes, he is still unable to observe it. Instead he sits downstairs and watches the death of Jip, the dog. He must still learn to accept responsibility for Dora's wished-for death, and, like Charles Darnay of *A Tale of Two Cities*, he must learn unheroically to accept the second life that her sacrifice has made possible for him. On the Yarmouth shore, after the self-sacrificing death of Ham Peggotty, another clown figure, or at least a "chuckle-headed" fellow, as Steerforth had called him, David is able to come a step closer to his selfhood and to the acceptance of death. In the last sentence of the novel, he is able finally to contemplate even his own demise.

This chain or, if you prefer, ladder of self-sacrifice—comic, sentimental, heroic—leads also to the disciplining of David Copperfield's heart, his ability to love Agnes not for his own gratification but for her own sake. It began, as we have seen, with Micawber, implausibly, according to the lights of many practical minded critics. Thus, J. B. Priestley:

> Indeed, the whole episode is preposterous. Uriah Heep would never have dreamed of employing such a person; Mr. Micawber would never have remained in the office a week; and even supposing that both actions were possible, he would never have been able to conceal his knowledge of Uriah's shady transactions or, what is yet more unlikely, have been able to ferret them all out, tabulate them in a formal document, and then bide his time until the proper moment for disclosure had arrived. Mr. Micawber as a financial detective is no more convincing than Shelley as a Bow Street runner.[35]

Similarly Mr. Lorry does not feel that Sydney Carton will be of much use in the crisis. Clearly David should perform the heroic act for himself. Clearly David should be allowed to become the hero of his own life, "a fine, firm fellow." So (Please, Mr. Dickens!) should we all be allowed, all of us fortunate

---

35. Priestley, *The English Comic Character*, pp. 240–41.

Harlequins. At the very least, we should not owe our lives and our loves to the self-sacrifice of a Clown, to the suicidal gesture of the drunkard Carton, to the absurd heroics of the soft Micawber. It is maddening and no more convincing to the unconverted reader than, so Priestley says, Shelley as a Bow Street runner or, according to a cynical W. H. Auden, than Shelley as the unacknowledged legislator of the world.[36] Yet in Dickens such clowns have a way of triumphing at the conclusion in spite of all the common sense that can be used by the Fitzjames Stephens of the world to refute them, and in that triumph, as the writer-priest would have it, lies our own salvation, for with Dickens and in the pantomime, poetry makes everything happen.

36. In "Writing," reprinted in *The Dyer's Hand and Other Essays* (New York: Random House, 1962), Auden wrote to contradict Shelley's claim that the poets are the unacknowledged legislators of the world: "The unacknowledged legislators of the world describes the secret police, not the poets" (p. 27). His more famous statement to a similar effect is, of course, the words from his elegy to Yeats: "Poetry makes nothing happen."

H. Brown, "Grimaldi's Farewell at Drury Lane," 1828.

Conclusion

The Death of the Clown

> Almost, at times, the Fool.
> —T. S. Eliot

The Clown's part in the pantomime was physically punishing, and Grimaldi, broken in body, his health shattered, had to retire from the stage a relatively young man. Thomas Hood wrote the following couplet as a comment on Grimaldi's son, who tried to succeed his father as the preeminent English Clown:

> Though Joseph Junior acts not ill,
> There's no fool like the old fool still.[1]

The son's end was sadder than the father's, for he was a derelict off stage as well as on, and, as Dickens pathetically recounted in both the *Memoirs of Joseph Grimaldi* and in the interpolated story of the dying clown in *Pickwick Papers*, he died a drunkard and in poverty.[2]

Many readers, especially readers of the 1850s and 1860s,

---

1. Extra illustrated edition of *Memoirs of Joseph Grimaldi* at the University of Texas Humanities Research Center. Hood is probably also the author of the following couplet regarding Dickens:

Arn't that ere Boz a tip-top feller!
Lots writes well, but he writes Weller!

although he ascribes the rhyme to "one of our Uneducated Poets." (*"Master Humphrey's Clock,"* Athenaeum, 7 November 1840, p. 887).

2. According to Kathleen Tillotson, Dickens based "The Stroller's Tale" on stories he knew about the death of Joseph Grimaldi, Jr. *The Letters of Charles Dickens* (Oxford: Oxford University Press, 1977), 4: 129n. He had not yet come into possession of the now lost manuscript of Grimaldi's memoirs, which he edited and largely rewrote.

Robert Seymour and Hablot Browne, "The Dying Clown," 1836, from *Pickwick Papers*. Courtesy of the University of California at Riverside Library.

Conclusion: The Death of the Clown 171

have felt about the Charles Dickens who wrote novels after *David Copperfield* much as Hood felt about the younger Grimaldi, although many others, especially in recent years, believe that the mature Dickens, the writer whom they regard as most worth a grown-up's attention, does not appear until this point. With *Bleak House*, the novel after *David Copperfield*, begins what has been called "the dark Dickens." Future generations will opt, as previous generations have done, for the Dickens that best suits their needs, but one thing is clear: there has been nothing like Wilkins Micawber either in Dickens or in English literature ever again.

It is impossible, of course, to say why the darkness fell, why Dickens' vision grew less hopeful or more realistic or more significant or however we want to describe the change, but one possible explanation is that five months after Dickens completed *David Copperfield*, with all its obsession with death and especially with the death of the father, his own father, John Dickens, died horribly. It was in the most uncomical manner imaginable, following unsuccessful surgery, performed without chloroform, for a bladder disease. Dickens called it "the most terrible operation known in surgery," and he described the room in which he saw his father immediately afterwards as "a slaughter house of blood."[3] One gruesome particular of the operation may be especially important in light of the powerful sexuality that commentators have traditionally associated with the pantomime Clown. As Robert Newsom explains, the operation not only mutilated and killed Dickens' father, it literally unsexed him by cutting a vagina-like "incision between the anus and the scrotum."[4] If John Dickens was indeed the model for Micawber and the Clowns of the earlier novels, as has been commonly assumed, it would be little wonder if this figure became lost or displaced in his son's creative imagination after 1851.

---

3. Letter to Mr. and Mrs. Dexter, 25 March 1851. Quoted in Edgar Johnson, *Charles Dickens: His Tragedy and Triumph*, 2 vols. (New York: Simon and Schuster, 1952), 2: 730–31.
4. Robert Newsom, *Dickens and the Romantic Side of Familiar Things* (New York: Columbia University Press, 1977), p. 161.

Although as I have said, Esther Summerson of *Bleak House* is the first in a line of truly interesting Columbines in Dickens' late works, it is impossible to designate a full complement of pantomime characters around her. There is a new character from the pantomime, the Malevolent Spirit, played by Miss Barbary, and John Jarndyce can be seen as a bumbling Benevolent Agent. Lady Dedlock is a meaningful variation of the troublesome Pantaloon, who allows all the mischief to be let loose. But Allan Woodcourt is perhaps the most admirable but certainly the least significantly interesting of all the Harlequins, and Esther is threatened by no Dandy Lover, interesting or otherwise, unless it is Mr. Guppy, who seems more accurately cast as the Clown. If so, Guppy appears to be the only Clown in a novel whose vision has transformed the angelic childishness of a Mr. Dick into the calculated innocence of a Skimpole and the courageous gentility of a Micawber into the blamably irresponsible deportment of a Turveydrop. If the magnificent Clowns of *David Copperfield* have indeed been reduced to a Guppy, then something has gone seriously wrong with the conception of this essential and dominating figure in the Dickens pantomime. The character in *Bleak House* who, like Newman Noggs and Dick Swiveller and Micawber, had "something in his manner, uncouth as it was, that denoted a fall in life" (chap. 11, p. 140), is Nemo, Esther's derelict father, and the words just quoted are spoken over his emaciated, opium-filled corpse. Like the earlier Clowns, Nemo serves the power of evil in the novel—he copies documents for Tulkinghorn—but we must not expect him to follow the others and imitate the pantomime Clown by rising up against his master. In fact, it is Tulkinghorn who discovers his dead body.

In the next novel, *Hard Times,* the pattern of pantomime characters reconstitutes itself to some extent. James Harthouse comes back from the melodrama to try his dandy wiles at seducing the Columbine, and Bounderby is another unsuitable lover, a veritable Squire Bugle from the Regency pantomime. Gradgrind, moreover, who puts Bounderby forth as a candidate for his daughter's hand, is one of the better and more meaningful Pantaloons in Dickens. But how disappointing a Clown is Sissy Jupe! And where is Louisa Gradgrind's Harlequin?

As we have already seen, the guilt-laden, nearly paralyzed suitable lover, or Harlequin, was to reappear with full credentials in both *Little Dorrit* and *A Tale of Two Cities* as Arthur Clennam and Charles Darnay. Moreover, Dickens had not finished his excruciating self-examination of this figure even then: Pip, John Harmon, and the vanished Edwin Drood were still to come. Dickens was not finished with the Pantaloon, either. William Dorrit, who, as Martin Meisel has shown, symbolically devours his daughter;[5] Dr. Manette, whose buried but resentful soul gives testimony to condemn his son-in-law and his grandchild; Magwitch; Miss Havisham; Mr. Podsnap; M.R.F.; and Old John Harmon, who menaces his son from a literal grave—all show that Dickens never forgave the hierarchy as embodied in the older, poisonous generation. He lost interest in Dandy Lovers for a while—Amy Dorrit is not at all troubled by such a character; Lawyer Stryver poses so weak a threat that he can be discouraged by a word from Mr. Lorry, and Bentley Drummle is one of the least interesting characters in *Great Expectations*—but Bradley Headstone and John Jasper are two of Dickens' most powerful and complex creations. Benevolent Agents make their supreme appearances on the stage of *Our Mutual Friend* and in the characters of Boffin and Jenny Wren.

Thus the pantomime continued to the end of Dickens' career, but the Clown, who was its principal and most powerful character, never seems to have recovered after *David Copperfield* and the death of John Dickens. Guppy is funny enough, but he's not much of a hero. Sissy Jupe redeems, but she's not very funny or very pathetic. She is defective, moreover, only according to Gradgrind's dim lights; from the schoolroom scene in the second chapter *we* always knew she was the healthiest character in the novel. The real Clown in *Hard Times*, Sissy's father, disappears and is never heard of again. John Chivery of *Little Dorrit* rises to heroic heights, or at least

---

5. Meisel, *Realizations*, p. 306.

to Mr. Tootsian heights, when he renounces his love for Amy and saves Clennam, his rival, but Chivery is obsessed by death and is preoccupied with the task of writing epitaphs for himself. Sydney Carton, as we have seen, is considerably more heroic, but his self-sacrifice on his rival's behalf leads to his own death.

Carton is the best Clown in Dickens after Micawber. He is a tragic Clown, but he may have been what Dickens was leading up to all the while. His Pierrot-like love for the heroine is easily as great as that of Tom Pinch or Mr. Toots, and it is clearly much more of a force to be reckoned with. The reader takes it and him seriously and wishes there were some way Lucie could reciprocate his commitment. Carton's dissipation, moreover, is clearly related to the worldview that *A Tale of Two Cities* tries to combat, whereas Newman Noggs was simply a country gentleman of irregular habits, who drank away his horses and hounds. Dick Swiveller is a sort of undergraduate. When Mrs. Micawber threw down the gauntlet and challenged the world to come forth and make some use of her obviously worthy husband, there was at least a Carlylean suggestion that something was wrong with an England which could provide no meaningful work for such a man, but it was only a suggestion. With Carton, however, it is clear that we are dealing with a man who is throwing his life away not only because of the "waste forces within him," but because of "the desert all around . . . the wilderness before him" (bk. 2, chap. 5, p. 85). In an age when the good men of Paris lie buried in the Bastille, and the best of the English, prematurely old, are interred in Tellson's underground bank, and where success comes only to the "always driving and riving and shouldering and pressing" Lawyer Stryver (bk. 2, chap. 5, p. 85), it is little wonder that Sydney Carton opts out.

Even more significantly, perhaps, Carton expresses the sexuality that was previously present in the Clown and the more attractive of the Dandy Lovers. If Carton belongs to the line of Clowns that began with Noggs, his Byronic languor suggests that he is also a meaningful sophistication of the melodramatic villain, Sir Mulberry Hawk, and that Steerforth and Harthouse and Gowan are Carton's ancestors, as well.[6] The two characters, Dandy Lover and Clown, were both played by Grimaldi and were never very far apart in Dickens' imagination, as witnessed by the fact that Dick Swiveller plays the one part in the first chapters of *The Old Curiosity Shop* before settling into the other for the remainder of the novel,[7] and that Mr. Toots is obsessed with his tailor and goes about with a prizefighter like a Regency buck, one of the Fancy, before romantically dedicating his life to Florence Dombey. In a way Sydney Carton is a conflation of Micawber and Steerforth, neither of whom can find proper and fulfilling work in England in the nineteenth century. "I have never learnt the art," says Steerforth, sounding like Carton, "of binding myself to any of the wheels on which the Ixions of these days are turning round and round" (p. 276). But Carton is also like Micawber in his ability to recognize the possibility of a redemption through self-sacrifice, inspired by and for the sake of the lady, "the only starry spot in . . . [Micawber's] miserable existence," the presence that makes Carton hear "whispers from old voices impelling me upward, that I thought were silent forever" (bk. 2, chap.13, p. 144). Like Micawber he acts heroically to save the lady, and like Steerforth he dies.

Sydney Carton's death saves Charles Darnay for Lucie Manette. There is even a suggestion in the conclusion that

---

6. Branwen Pratt, in "Carlyle and Dickens" (see chap. 1, n. 43), relates Carton and Wrayburn to Lord Frederick and Dick Swiveller, but also to Steerforth and Harthouse, "Dickens' familiar dandiacal, semi-Byronic, perversely attractive, slightly Bohemian, somewhat wicked aristocrat[s]," p. 243.

7. Thomas Hood's initial reaction upon encountering Swiveller in the pages of *Master Humphrey's Clock* is instructive in this regard:

> There are thousands of Swivellers growing, or grown up, about town; neglected, ill-conditioned profligates, who owe their misconduct not to a bad bringing up but to having had no bringing up at all. Human hulks, cast loose on the world with no more pilotage than belongs to mere brute intelligence—like abandoned hulls that are found adrift at sea, with only a monkey on board. Such a derelict is Dick Swiveller—a fellow of easy virtue and easy vice—lax, lounging, and low, in morals and habits, and living on from day to day by a series of shifts and shabbinesses. . . . Still there is more of folly than of absolute vice about Richard Swiveller. (*"Master Humphrey's Clock,"* p. 888)

Grimaldi as My Lord Humpy Dandy in *Harlequin Munchausen*, 1818. Courtesy of David Mayer III.

Conclusion: The Death of the Clown 177

Carton's act of self-sacrifice may have redeemed a selfish world and made possible a Paris of beautiful people and a London in which Lucie's son can honorably aspire to an illustrious career in the law. But it was a real death within Dickens' creative imagination, for Carton is the last of the Clowns. In *Great Expectations* this figure is entirely absent for the first time in a Dickens novel. Perhaps as a result, in the first draft at least, the hero does not win the heroine, also for the first time in a Dickens novel.[8] There are two happy endings in *Our Mutual Friend,* the last novel that Dickens completed. In one of the plots, a Harlequin, John Harmon, comes back from the dead, and in the other, a Dandy Lover, Eugene Wrayburn, marries the lower-class heroine he had penultimately resolved to make his mistress. It is all very wonderful, but there are no proper Clowns, and the redemptions are almost entirely the work of the Benevolent Agents. Noddy Boffin and Jenny Wren are perhaps the best fairy godparents in Dickens, and Boffin's pious fraud is certainly the most elaborate piece of deceptive, pantomimic magic in all the novels, but without the Clown some readers have remained unconvinced.

The loss of the Clown has perhaps served to make Dickens' works more accessible to our age, which has a hard time respecting literature that is not realistically pessimistic, and which resents authorial attempts to improve the reader's character. It was, however, a serious blow to Dickens' moral aesthetics, one that laid him open to the objections of socially oriented critics, both conservative and Marxist, who complain that he was good at pointing out the faults and injustices of the system but stopped short of pointing out constructive remedies, that he timidly counseled against revolution but could devise no way of altering the hearts of people so that they

---

8. I have dealt with this topic at much greater length in "The Absent Clown in *Great Expectations,*" *Dickens Studies Annual* 11, ed. Michael Timko, Fred Kaplan, and Edward Guiliano (New York: AMS Press, 1983), pp. 115–33. There is, of course, no marriage for the principal heroine of *Hard Times* either, but this is Dickens' novel without a hero.

could change society without violence. The pantomime Clown and Benevolent Agent, working at cross-purposes somehow together, seemed to provide that way of changing hearts and souls, but when the Clown was lost, an essential part of the aesthetics disappeared. Although the Good Fairy was still possible, she had been imported into the pantomime from children's literature, where she still really belonged. It was easy for grown-ups to dismiss her as a dreamy embodiment of wish-fulfillment. The wild, anarchical Clown, however, was born in the bawdry of the English pantomime, and while panto has become more and more over the years a species of children's theater, it was much less so in Dickens' youth. Even today a typical pantomime audience is composed of people of all ages, and a considerable number of the spectators have not brought the children along.[9]

It is difficult to say whether modern audiences find the paradise that the Victorians looked for at the pantomime, but if they do, I suspect it is a more materialistic business altogether, for the transformations nowadays are entirely of scenery and never of character, and there is no harlequinade anymore. But the stage magic that enthralled the young Charles Dickens and that he tried to tap for the sake of his highly moral art is still around. The novels of Dickens and the Christmas pantomime, moreover, remain two of England's most popular and morally influential artistic expressions.

9. The newspaper advertisements of the Riverside [California] Civic Light Opera Company, an American repertory that regularly stages pantomimes, advises audiences to exercise parental discretion.

Index

à Beckett, Gilbert, 4
Absurdism, 3, 8–11, 19, 102, 167
Actors and acting, ix, 4–5, 155n12, 156–157, 159, 169; and gender switching, 123, 125–126; and status of character, 144
Addison, Joseph, 55
Adrian, Arthur A., 74
Aladdin, 126
All the Year Round (periodical), 3n6, 5, 16, 42, 70
Alter, Robert, 109n8
Anarchy, 9, 41, 44–45, 154–156, 178
Anastaplo, George, 165n34
Aristophanes, 19
Aristotle, 22
As You Like It (Shakespeare), 14, 163–164
Auden, W. H., 167, 167n36
Audience, ix, 13–15, 23, 47, 65, 68, 105, 123, 125, 178; and genre, 25, 40–41; and harlequinade, 3, 11, 67, 70, 155; and *ressentiment*, 101; and transformation scene, 44
Autobiography, 49, 108n6, 117
Axton, William, 6n15, 11, 24–25, 29

Bad Baron, 26
Bakhtin, Mikhail, 10, 11, 12, 14, 16n42, 21, 41, 162
Balzac, Honoré de, 33, 37, 39
Barickman, Richard, 131n3
Bartholomew Fair, 12
Bartholomew Fair (Jonson), 13
Beard, Thomas, 54n14
Beckett, Samuel, 165
Benevolent Agent, x, 8, 32, 45; Nicodemus Boffin as, 55, 67, 173, 177; Cheeryble brothers as, 17, 49, 67; John Jarndyce as, 55, 67, 172; Julia Mills as, 76; Pickwick as, 8; and pious fraud, 55, 57, 62, 67, 137, 141; relation with Clown, 178; and sexuality, 47; and transformation scene, 41, 47, 104, 123; Betsey Trotwood as, 47, 49, 55, 64, 67, 83, 121, 141, 147; Lord Frederick Verisopht as, 18; Jenny Wren as, 173, 177
Bentley's Miscellany (periodical), 5, 12, 109
Bildungsroman, 51, 65–66. *See also* Novel of development, English
Blanchard, E. L., 4
Bolton, H. Philip, 6
Booth, Bradford, 59n24
Booth, Michael, 9, 23–24, 154–155
Bossu, René Le, 22
Bristol, Michael D., 41
Brontë, Emily, 127
Brooks, Peter, 33–34, 39
Brough, Robert, 4
Browne, Hablot K. ("Phiz"), 107–108
Buckstone, John Baldwin, 4, 26, 39
Bulwer-Lytton, Edward, 60, 128
Burlesque, 7, 11, 22, 25, 163
Buttons, 137, 144
Butwin, Joseph, 6n15
Byron, George Gordon, sixth baron, 97, 101, 120, 174

Carabine, Keith, 134n5
Carlyle, Thomas, 51, 59, 65–66, 91, 120, 127, 161, 174
Carnivalesque, 10–11, 13–14, 16n42, 41, 68, 164
Cavell, Stanley, 63

179

Chaplin, Charlie, 24, 102, 157
Chapman, Raymond, 162
Characters, x, 16–18; author identified with, 107–109; comic, xi, 11, 69–70, 102, 147, 156–157, 159–160; and faulty hero, 67; and gender, 41, 95, 116–117, 123, 125–129, 131, 137, 141, 146; identification with, 107–111, 116, 125, 128, 136–139, 141–142; as illuminators of culture, 40; and interchange of genres, 93, 102; and melodrama, 26, 93, 102, 127, 143–144; in mimetic fiction, 156; in modern pantomime, 47; and moral development, 57, 60, 68, 84, 121, 142, 145, 164, 166; moral development of, 51–55, 65–66, 137–139, 177; motivation of, 83, 118; and pantomime, 2, 11, 14–16, 26, 69, 93, 102, 127, 143–144; and pious fraud, 62, 67; and plot, 2, 93, 102; proletarian, 87–88; psychology of, 8, 135–136; and realism, 50–51, 55, 57; and role reversal, 41; upper-class, 93. *See also* Heroes; Heroines; Villains
Chesterton, Gilbert Keith, xi, 20, 33, 50, 107, 109, 111, 117, 129, 139, 143, 157, 161, 163
Childe Harold (Byron), 120
Chittick, Kathryn, 6n17
Cinderella, 126, 144
Cinderella story, 136–137
Cinema, 24, 33
Class, social, 93–100, 106, 118, 152, 155, 177
Clinton-Baddeley, V. C., 126–127
Clown, x, 2–3, 6n15, 13–16, 20, 23, 45, 68, 70, 76, 121; as anarchic figure, 152, 154, 156, 164, 178; as Buttons, 144; Sydney Carton as, 19, 145, 148, 157, 174; John Chivery as, 145, 173–174; David Copperfield as, 149–150; Dandy Lover changed to, 91; and death theme, 148–149, 151, 157, 160, 164–165; Mr. Dick as, 147; Dickens' father as model for, 171, 173; Martha Endell as, 157; Fagin as, 72; Mr. Guppy as, 145, 172–173; as hero, 142, 157, 160, 166, 173, 175; immorality of, 146–147, 159; Sissy Jupe as, 146, 173; as master of speech, 160–161; Wilkins Micawber as, xi–xii, 19, 150, 157, 160–167, 174; and morality, 20, 41; narrative status of, 144; as Nemesis, 148; Nemo as, 172; Newman Noggs as, 17, 19, 26–27, 93, 156; Kit Nubbles as, 18–19, 145; Pecksniff as, 72; physical demands on, 169; Mr. Pickwick as, 72; as Pierrot, 144–145, 149, 156n12, 174; Tom Pinch as, 73, 145; and problem of gender, 146; and realism, 142; relation with Benevolent Agent, 178; relation with Columbine, 143–144, 156; relation with Dandy Lover, 150, 154, 175; relation with Harlequin, 156, 160–161, 167; relation with heroine, 143–145, 146, 149; relation with Pantaloon, 70, 72, 74, 151–152, 154, 156; relation with villain, 150, 152; as rescuer, 145–149, 157, 161–162; as ruling figure, xi; as saturnalian spirit, 10, 152; Scrooge as, 72; self-sacrifice of, 145, 147, 164, 166, 175, 177; and serious literature, 40; and sexuality, 171, 174; Smike as, 145; and social critique, 154–155, 162–163; Dora Spenlow as, 139n10, 141; Dick Swiveller as, 19–20, 146, 148, 156–157, 160; Mr. Toots as, 32, 145; tragic, xii; Job Trotter as, 8; Lord Frederick Verisopht as, 19, 93, 147; Sam Weller as, 7–8; Jenny Wren as, 146
Cockshut, A. O. J., xi, 50, 99
Coleridge, Samuel Taylor, 108
Collins, Wilkie, 55n14, 110, 112
Columbine, x, 2–3, 11, 13, 15, 26, 67–68, 91, 101, 104, 110, 120–121, 129, 148, 152, 172; Madeline Bray as, 130; David Copperfield as, 141; Louisa Gradgrind as, 172; Kate Nickleby as, 17–18; passivity of, 130; Miss Rachel as, 7; relation

with Clown, 143–144, 156; Dora Spenlow as, 76; Esther Summerson as, 172; as victim, 151; Agnes Wickfield as, 135, 141
Comédie-Française, 1n2
Comedy, 2–3, 19, 21, 32, 44, 64, 70, 102, 104, 121, 152, 163; and characters, xi, 11, 69–70, 102, 147, 156–157, 159–160; cosmic implications of, 9; and pantomime, xi, 3, 8–9, 11; and realism, 23–24; and social critique, 11; as vehicle of protest, 38–39
Commedia dell'arte, 119
Confidence-Man (Melville), 40
Conrad, Joseph, 33
Cope, Jackson, 149
Costume, 11, 22–23, 41, 93
Courtly love, 136, 149
Craik, Mrs. (Dinah Maria Mulock), 127
Crick, Brian, 85, 87
Criticism: American school of Dickensian, xi, 136; and author-character identification, 107–109; feminist, 35, 131, 133; Freudian, 127n27; and genre, 21, 26; golden rule of, 108; and harlequinade, 3; Marxist, 34, 127n27, 177; and panto's influence on Dickens, 5–12; psychological, xi; realist, 55, 57; of society, 11–12, 34–36, 39, 41, 44, 60, 93–95, 101, 154, 162–163, 177–178; symbolic, xi
Cruikshank, George, 24

Dame, 47, 49
Dandy (or Wicked) Lover, x, 2, 24, 26; as authority figure, 154; James Carker as, 93; disappearance from panto, 91; Bentley Drummle as, 94, 173; Arthur Gride as, 17, 73, 91, 93; Mr. Guppy as, 172; James Harthouse as, 172; Sir Mulberry Hawk as, 17, 73, 93, 94; Bradley Headstone as, 173; Uriah Heep as, 98–102; John Jasper as, 173; Jack Maldon as, 100; and melodrama, 93, 96, 98, 101; Edward Murdstone as, 141; Ralph Nickleby as, 148; Daniel Quilp as, 19, 101–102; relation with Clown, 150, 154, 175; as rescuer, 148; satirical function of, 91, 93; and sexuality, 174; and social class, 93–101; James Steerforth as, 95–98, 141; Lawyer Stryver as, 173; Dick Swiveller as, 18; Mr. Tupman as, 7, 17; as victim, 101; as villain, 91, 93–94, 98, 101, 104; Red Whisker as, 76; Eugene Wrayburn as, 177
Dante Alighieri, 85
Dark Scene, 2, 8, 11, 32, 83, 152
Davis, Earle, 32–33, 57n20, 61–62
Death theme, 75, 77, 86, 95, 174; and Clown, 148–149, 151, 157, 160, 164–165; and death of Dickens' father, 171, 173; and gentility, 78–79, 89–90, 96, 98–99, 101, 119, 133; and harlequinade, 121
Deburau, Jean-Baptiste, 144–145
Dewey, Jane, 25n12
Dibden, Tom, 26, 105, 130
Dickens, Charles: and blacking warehouse incident, 115; change of values, xi, 16, 35, 171; childhood experience of panto, 3–4, 69, 178; collaboration with Collins, 110, 112; dandy manners of, 91; as editor of *Bentley's Miscellany*, 12–13; encounters with panto actors, 4–5; identified with his protagonists, 107–109; and illustrator's mistake, 66n33; Maclise portrait of, 107; relation with father, 69, 171, 173; relation with mother, 80; relation with sister-in-law, 111, 130; self-regard of, 59–60; theatrical activity of, 159; views on serious literature, 59–60, 66–67; views on sexuality of, 84–85; writings on panto by, 5, 13–16, 69, 73n10, 109–110, 121, 160

WORKS

Barnaby Rudge, 35, 55n16, 74, 80, 121, 150
Battle of Life, 55, 66, 139

Dickens, Charles (*continued*)
  Bleak House, 26, 30–31, 55, 67, 74, 77, 91, 110, 121, 123, 126, 131, 134, 145, 150, 172; death theme in, 164; and Dickens' change of values, 171–172; guilt theme in, 113; heroines in, 131, 172; novel writing as an art in, 59; social critique in, 34; villains in, 26
  Chimes, 49 n2, 55
  Christmas Books, 142
  Christmas Carol, 12, 46, 55, 58, 72, 112, 121, 162
  Cricket on the Hearth, 55, 82
  David Copperfield, x–xii, 5, 16, 19, 30–32, 39, 40, 46, 49–55, 61–65, 67, 74–90, 94–102, 104–108, 110–111, 116–121, 125–128, 130, 133–139, 141, 143, 146–152, 157, 159–167, 171–172, 174–175; adapted for theater, 72 n5; as autobiography, 49, 117; as *Bildungsroman*, 51–52, 65; character development in, 50–55, 65–66, 84, 95, 121, 164, 166; comic characters in, xi–xii, 102, 159–160; Dark Scene in, 152; denouement in, 64–65; and Dickens' change of values, xi, 171; faith versus skepticism in, 62–64, 86–87; and fantasy, 50; gentility as motif in, 77–79, 87–90, 94, 96–97, 101, 118–119, 133–134, 151, 159; and happy ending, 161–163; harlequinade in, 120; idea of death in, 75, 77–79, 86, 89–90, 95–96, 98–99, 101, 119, 133, 148–149, 151, 157, 164–166, 171; interchange of genres in, 46, 52, 61, 102; marriage theme in, 77, 85, 95, 99, 107–108; moral center of, 49; parent-child relations in, 79–80; pious fraud in, 52–55, 61–62, 64–67, 141–142; problem of genre in, 125–128; protagonist's doubles in, 99–100; protagonist's guilt in, 117, 119–121, 138–139; protagonist's unheroic nature in, 105–107, 125–126; and realism, 50; sexuality in, 134–135; social aspiration in, 94–99, 118, 148; villains in, 74
  Dombey and Son, 26, 29, 30, 32, 34–35, 39, 72–73, 80, 92, 94, 100–101, 108, 110–112, 121, 123, 133, 145–146, 152, 174–175; Dark Scene in, 32; death scene in, 165; heroes in, 111–112; heroines in, 133, 141 n11; hopeless love in, 145; illustrations for, 109; interchange of genres in, 28–30; parent-child relation in, 80; social aspiration in, 100; villains in, 26, 72–73
  Frozen Deep (with Wilkie Collins), 110
  Great Expectations, x, 5, 26, 31–32, 67, 94, 99, 108, 110–111, 117, 121, 134, 173, 177
  Hard Times, 31–32, 35, 67, 76 n14, 80 n17, 146, 172–173, 175
  Little Dorrit, 30, 31, 67, 80, 85 n21, 91, 113, 115, 117, 121, 134, 142, 145, 151, 173–175; guilt theme in, 113, 115; interchange of genres in, 30–32; parent-child relation in, 80; social critique in, 34
  Martin Chuzzlewit, 72–73, 80, 83, 94, 104, 110–112, 121, 133, 145–146, 150, 157, 160, 174
  Master Humphrey's Clock, '18, 175 n7
  Memoirs of Joseph Grimaldi, 4–5, 14, 69, 148, 169
  Mystery of Edwin Drood, 5, 39, 121, 173
  Nicholas Nickleby, 5, 16, 17–19, 25 n14, 26–28, 34, 49, 67, 73–75, 80, 91, 93–94, 99, 108, 110–112, 118, 121, 123, 130–131, 145–148, 150, 156, 172, 174, 175 n6; as autobiography, 108 n6; gentility as motif in, 93–94; heroines in, 130; interchange of genres in, 26–29, 93; parent-child relation in, 75, 80; pious fraud in, 67; satire in, 25, villains in, 73, 99

No Thoroughfare (with Wilkie Collins), 112–113
Old Curiosity Shop, 16, 18–19, 38, 67, 84, 91, 101–102, 121, 130, 135, 145–146, 148, 150, 156–157, 160, 172, 174–175
Oliver Twist, 35, 37, 72, 78–79, 83, 108, 111–113, 123, 125, 133
Our Mutual Friend, 30–32, 49n2, 54–55, 57n20, 58, 62, 64, 67, 75, 82, 84, 100–101, 112, 117, 121, 131, 133–134, 142, 146, 173–177; happy ending in, 177; heroines in, 131, 142; interchange of genres in, 30–32; parent-child relation in, 74–75, 82, 84; pious fraud in, 54, 57–58, 64; social class in, 100
Pickwick Papers, 7–8, 49n2, 72, 107, 111, 120–121, 157, 159
Sketches by Boz, 5, 24
Tale of Two Cities, x, 5–6, 16, 19, 28, 31–32, 35, 39, 74, 106, 109–110, 113, 115–116, 145, 147–148, 150, 157, 162, 166–167, 173–175, 177; and French Revolution, 35; protagonist's unheroic nature in, 105–107, 109–110, 113, 115–117, 166, 173, 175

CHARACTERS

Bagstock, Major Joey, 30
Barbary, Miss, 172
Bardell, Mrs., 107
Barkis, 165
Biddy, 111
Blackpool, Stephen, 32
Boffin, Nicodemus, 31–32, 49n2, 54–55, 57n20, 62, 64, 67, 173, 177
Bounderby, Josiah, 80n17, 172
Bray, Madeline, 17, 26, 28, 75, 111, 130–131, 146
Bray, Walter, 80
Brooker, 148, 156
Browdie, John, 27
Brown, Good Mrs., 80
Bucket, Inspector, 31
Buzfuz, Sergeant, 107
Carker, Harriet, 133

Carker, James, 26, 29, 32, 39, 72–73, 92, 94, 100–101, 133, 152
Carton, Sydney, 16, 19, 28, 32, 35, 74, 106, 109–110, 113, 116, 145, 147–148, 150, 157, 166–167, 174–175, 177
Cheeryble Brothers, 17, 28, 49, 67, 145
Chester, John, 80
Chivery, John, 30, 145, 151, 173–174
Chuzzlewit, Jonas, 18
Chuzzlewit, Young Martin, 94, 110–112, 121, 133
Claypole, Noah, 125
Clennam, Arthur, 30, 113, 115, 117, 121, 173
Copperfield, Clara, 85, 98, 135
Copperfield, David, 5, 30, 32, 46, 50–54, 61–65, 67, 76–78, 82–83, 87–89, 94, 97–101, 102, 105–107, 108, 110–111, 116–121, 125–128, 133–134, 136, 138, 141, 149–151, 164–165
Copperfield, Dora (Spenlow), 30, 32, 53, 76, 79, 107, 117, 119, 135, 138–139, 141, 146–147, 149–150, 164, 166
Creakle, Miss, 118, 135
Creakle, Mr., 75
Crummles, Vincent, 28
Cruncher, Jerry, 116
Curdle, Mr., 25n14
Cuttle, Captain Edward, 32
Darnay, Charles, 31, 105–107, 109–110, 113, 115–117, 145, 166, 173, 175
Dartle, Rosa, 97, 126, 135
Dedlock, Lady, 30–31, 172
Defarge, Madame, 35, 39, 106, 115
Dick, Mr., 64, 147, 150, 164–165, 172
Dolls, Mr., 31, 84
Dombey, Edith, 30, 80, 133
Dombey, Florence, 32, 111, 145
Dombey, Mr., 34–35, 100
Dombey, Paul, 30, 123
Dorrit, Amy, 31, 67, 85n21, 134, 173

Dickens, Charles (*continued*)
  Dorrit, William, 31, 80, 173
  Drood, Edwin, 121, 173
  Drummle, Bentley, 94, 173
  Endell, Martha, 87, 134–135, 148–149, 157
  Estella, 99
  Fagin, 35, 72
  Fat Boy, 7
  Folair, Mr., 5
  Gamp, Sarah, 108, 157, 160
  Gargery, Joe, 94, 111
  Gay, Walter, 94, 108, 110–112, 121, 133, 145
  Gowan, Henry, 30, 67, 91, 175
  Gradgrind, Louisa, 31, 76n14, 80n17, 146, 173
  Gradgrind, Thomas, 76n14, 80n17, 172–173
  Graham, Mary, 73, 111, 146
  Gride, Arthur, 17, 73–74, 91, 93, 99
  Grimwig, Mr., 83
  Grub, Gabriel, 121
  Gummidge, Mrs., 89, 135
  Guppy, William, 31, 74, 145, 150, 172
  Harmon, John, 30, 112, 121, 133, 173, 177
  Harthouse, James, 76n14, 172, 175
  Havisham, Miss, 173
  Hawk, Sir Mulberry, 26, 28, 73, 93–94, 99, 150, 174
  Headstone, Bradley, 31, 100–101, 112, 173
  Heep, Mrs., 98, 135
  Heep, Uriah, 30, 32, 39, 63, 74–76, 83, 86, 98, 100–102, 104, 108, 117, 126, 134n5, 146, 151–152, 160–161, 164–166
  Hexam, Lizzie, 75, 112
  Humphrey, Master, 18
  Jarley, Mrs., 67
  Jarndyce, John, 55, 67
  Jasper, John, 39, 173
  Jingle, Alfred, 7–8, 111, 120
  Jo, 30–31, 123
  Joram, 99
  Jorkins, Mr., 99
  Jupe, Sissy, 146, 173
  La Creevy, Miss, 67
  Larkins, Miss, 117, 135
  Lightwood, Mortimer, 112
  Littimer, 100, 133, 134n5
  Little Dick, 78, 113
  Little Em'ly, 64, 67, 78, 86–90, 94–99, 117–118, 126, 133–135, 138, 148–149, 151
  Little Nell, 38, 84, 101–102, 130, 135, 145–146
  Magwitch, Abel, 31, 99, 173
  Maldon, Jack, 61–62, 100, 110–111, 135
  Manette, Dr., 115–116, 173
  Manette, Lucie, 175, 177
  Markleham, Mrs., 75–76, 79–80, 82–84, 86
  Marley, Jacob, 58
  Marwood, Alice, 133
  Maylie, Harry, 111
  Maylie, Rose, 78, 113
  Meagles, Pet, 30, 85n21
  Mell, Mr., 88, 96, 117–118
  Merdle, Mr., 31
  Micawber, Mrs., 134, 174
  Micawber, Wilkins, xi–xii, 16, 19, 32, 40, 74–75, 105, 107, 126, 143, 146, 150–152, 157, 159–165, 166–167, 171–172, 174–175
  Mills, Julia, 76
  Mowcher, Miss, 134
  Murdstone, Edward, 75, 95–96, 125, 134–135, 141, 151, 164
  Murdstone, Jane, 116
  Nancy, 37, 78, 113, 133
  Nemo, 172
  Nickleby, Kate, 17–18, 28, 73, 94n2, 118, 145, 147
  Nickleby, Mrs., 80, 118
  Nickleby, Nicholas, 5, 17, 73, 94n2, 110–111, 118, 121
  Nickleby, Ralph, 17, 27–28, 34, 73, 93, 94n2, 108, 112, 146, 148, 150, 156
  Nipper, Susan, 145
  Noggs, Newman, 17, 19, 26–27, 73, 146, 148, 150, 156, 172, 174
  Nubbles, Kit, 18–19, 121, 145, 150
  Omer, Minnie, 134

Omer, Mr., 75, 88–89, 99
Pecksniff, Seth, 72–73, 79–80, 82–86, 98–99, 173
Peerybingle, John, 82
Peggotty, Clara, 75, 87, 135
Peggotty, Daniel, 76, 86–90, 149
Peggotty, Ham, 87, 89, 96, 148–149, 166
Pickwick, Samuel, 7, 72, 107, 121, 159
Pinch, Tom, 73, 111, 145–146, 150, 174
Pip, 5, 67, 94, 99, 111, 117, 121, 134, 173
Podsnap, Mr., 58, 173
Pross, Miss, 32
Pumblechook, Uncle, 110
Quilp, Daniel, 19, 91, 101, 135, 150
Quilp, Mrs., 91
Red Whisker, 76
Rob the Grinder, 72, 152
Rudge, Barnaby, 55 n16, 150
Scrooge, Ebenezer, 72, 112, 121
Sharp, Mr., 118
Shepherd, Miss, 135
Sikes, Bill, 79, 108, 112, 133
Skewton, Mrs., 30, 80
Skimpole, Harold, 172
Sleary, 67
Smike, 28, 73, 94 n2, 123, 145, 147
Snagsby, Mrs., 31
Sparsit, Mrs., 31
Spenlow, Mr., 74–79, 87, 89, 99, 119
Squeers, 28
Steerforth, James, 30, 32, 64, 67, 75, 78, 87–88, 94–96, 99–101, 117–119, 125, 127, 133, 135, 138, 141, 149–151, 164, 166, 174–175
Steerforth, Mrs., 85, 97–98, 135
Strong, Annie, 30–31, 51, 61–65, 82–83, 85, 87, 100, 110, 135, 137–139, 147
Strong, Dr., 46, 82, 85, 149
Stryver, 74, 106, 173–174
Summerson, Esther, 126, 131, 134, 172
Swiveller, Dick, 16, 146, 148, 150, 156–157, 160, 172, 174–175
Tattycoram, 142
Toots, Mr., 32, 111, 145–146, 174–175
Traddles, Tommy, 75, 141
Trent, Mr., 19, 84
Trotter, Job, 7–8, 49 n2
Trotwood, Betsey, 46, 49–53, 54–55, 64–65, 67, 83, 116, 134, 138–139, 141, 147, 164
Tulkinghorn, Mr., 26, 31, 74, 172
Tupman, Mr., 7
Turveydrop, Mr., 91, 172
Turveydrop, Prince, 126
Twist, Oliver, 78, 113, 123, 125, 133
Veck, Trotty, 49 n2
Verisopht, Lord Frederick, 16, 19, 28, 93, 147, 150, 156, 175 n6
Vholes, Mr., 31
Wardle, Miss Rachel, 7
Wardle, Mr., 7
Wardour, Richard, 110
Weller, Sam, 7, 157
Wickfield, Agnes, 30, 51, 54, 63–65, 82–87, 99, 102, 111, 130, 135–137, 139, 141, 150, 164, 166
Wickfield, Mr., 61, 63–64, 74, 76, 84–87, 89 n25, 98, 100
Wilding, Walter, 112–113
Wilfer, Bella, 30, 54, 82, 112, 131, 134, 142
Willet, Joe, 121
Willet, John, 74
Woodcourt, Allan, 110, 121, 172
Wrayburn, Eugene, 31–32, 100, 112, 117, 121, 175 n6, 177
Wren, Jenny, 146, 173, 177
Dickens, John, 16, 69, 171
Disraeli, Benjamin, 127
Donne, John, 63
Dostoevsky, Feodor, 33–34
Dragon of Wantley, 74
Duchess of Malfi (Webster), 33
Dunn, Richard, 51

Educational method, 52–54
Edwards, Michael, 160
Eigner, Edwin M., 131 n4, 177
Eliot, T. S., 169

Elizabethan period, 19
Emile (Rousseau), 53
Euripides, 33

Fairy tale, 23, 41–42, 47, 67, 120, 136, 138, 159–160, 178
Falstaff, 157, 159–160
Fantasy, 11, 16, 23–25, 50, 55, 58, 121, 136
Farley, Charles, 23, 120
Fielding, Henry, 51, 57n19
Fields, W. C., 157
Findlater, Richard, 10, 144, 152
Fitzgerald, Percy, 42
Flexmore, Richard, 155n12
Forster, John, 83
Frank, Lawrence, 106
Franklin, Stephen L., 49
French Revolution, 34–35, 93, 174
Freud, Sigmund, 75
Frow, Gerald, 1n2, 22n3
Frye, Northrop, 8–10, 11, 19, 44–45, 70

Garis, Robert, 55–57
Garrick, David, x
Gautier, Théophile, 119, 155n12
Gender, 46, 95, 116–117, 131, 137, 141, 146; switching of, 41, 47, 123, 125–127
Genre, 143; and character development, 52; and comedy, 32, 38; and melodrama, 25–30, 32, 36, 38, 93, 102; and pantomime, 22, 25–30, 32, 93, 102; and realism, 39; shift of, 25–30, 32, 38–39, 45–46, 61, 93, 102; and tragedy, 63; and villains, 102; and worldview, 21–22, 26, 32
Gentility, concept of, 77–79, 87–89, 93–94, 96–97, 101, 118–119, 133–134, 159
Gilbert, Elliot, 109n8
Gillray, James, 24
Goethe, Johann Wolfgang von, 51, 54, 65–67
Gogol, Nikolai, 33
Goldsmith, Oliver, 38, 57
Gomme, A. H., 106–107
Good Fairy, 2, 7–8

Good Natured Man (Goldsmith), 57
Gothic fiction, 101, 105, 144
Grand Transformation, 41–42, 44, 47, 60–61
Grimaldi, Joseph, 2, 4, 6, 8, 10, 17–19, 24, 120–121, 143–144, 148–149, 152, 154, 157, 159, 169, 175
Grimaldi, Joseph, Jr., 169–171
Grotesque, 10–12, 25
Guy, Earl of Harrick, or, Harlequin and the Dun Cow (Morton), 23n5
Guy Livingstone (Lawrence), 127

Halliday, Andrew, 2, 3n6, 68–72
Hamlet (Shakespeare), 21, 126n24
Hansel and Gretel, 47
Happy ending, 44, 104, 161, 177
Hardy, Barbara, 135, 136
Harlequin, x, 2–3, 5, 11, 13, 15–16, 22–23, 67–68, 70, 83, 104–105, 130, 148, 152; Frank Cheeryble as, 17–18; Arthur Clennam as, 173; and comedy, 121; David Copperfield as, 76, 135, 141, 165; Charles Darnay as, 173, 175; Edwin Drood as, 173; as everyman, 109–110; Guy Fawkes as, 120; and gender, 123, 125, 129; as guilt-laden character, 119–121, 151, 173; John Harmon as, 173, 177; as hero, 94; Alfred Jingle as, 7–8, 120; Nicholas Nickleby as, 17; Kit Nubbles as, 18; Peeping Tom as, 120; Pip as, 173; relation with Clown, 156, 160–161, 167; and sexuality, 123, 125; and transformation scene, 41–42; Agnes Wickfield as, 141, Allan Woodcourt as, 172
Harlequinade, 3, 6–7, 12, 22; and anarchy, 9, 11; and Clown, 144, 148, 151, 154; and death theme, 121; disappearance of, 47, 178; expiatory function of, 67, 120–121; in French panto, 144; and Pantaloon, 69–70; and realism, 16, 23–24; violence in, 102
Harlequin and Cinderella, 144
Harlequin and Guy Fawkes; or, The Fifth of November, 120n17
Harlequin and Mother Bunch; or, The Yellow Dwarf (Farley), 23n5

Harlequin and Mother Goose (Dibden), 130
Harlequin and the Elfin Arrow; or, The Basket Maker and His Brother, 70n4
Harlequin and the King of Clubs; or, The Knave who Stole the Syllabub, 70n4
Harlequin and the Ogress (Farley), 23n5
Harlequin Peeping Tom of Coventry, 120n17
Harlequin's Chaplet, 91
Hazlitt, William, 127
Heath, William, 24
Heilman, Robert B., 33, 36
Henry V (in Shakespeare's *Henry IV, Part 1*), 139
Heroes, 105, 109–110, 118, 120, 145, 157, 160, 166, 173, 177; defective nature of, 105–107, 125–126, 147; guilt feeling of, 111–113, 115, 119–121, 134, 138–139; moral development of, 137–139; narrative status of, 143–144; and problem of gender, 95, 116–117, 123, 125–129, 141, 146; and sexuality, 128–129
Heroines, 49, 75, 85, 128, 177; and expiation of guilt, 133–134; liberation of, 131, 133; in melodrama, 143; moral development of, 137; narrative status of, 133; relation with Clown, 143–146, 149; relation with villains, 143; and religion, 131, 136; and sexuality, 133; symbolic status of, 136; as victims, 131
Hobbes, Thomas, 84
Hogarth, Mary, 111, 130
Hollington, Michael, 5–6, 10n26, 24, 72
Hood, Thomas, 169, 171, 175n7
Hornback, Bert G., 141n11
House, Humphry, 162, 163
Household Words (periodical), 5, 15
Howells, W. D., 57
Hume, David, 38
Humpty Dumpty, 159–160
Hunchback, The (Knowles), 57n20
Hunt, Leigh, 9, 143

Identification: with protagonist, 107–111, 116, 125, 128, 136–139, 141–142
Idylls of the King (Tennyson), 128–129
In Memoriam (Tennyson), 127
Institutions, fictional, 34, 77

Jack and the Beanstalk, 123n20
Jack and the Beanstalk (Morley), 49n2
James, Henry, 33, 39
Jeaffreson, J. C., 55
Jerdan, William, 12–13
John Halifax, Gentleman (Craik), 127
Johnson, James, 155n12
Johnson's Account of Pantomime, 155n12
Jones, Louisa E., 10, 28
Jonson, Ben, 9, 13
Jordan, John O., 87n24, 118
Joyce, James, x, 120n17
Julius Caesar (Shakespeare), 67

Kaplan, Fred, 38, 44
Keats, John, 16n42
Kensick, Helen Lorraine, 6n15, 27n17
Kettle, Arnold, 35, 97
Kincaid, James R., 72, 126, 157, 162–164
Knowles, Sheridan, 57n20
Kotzebue, August von, 80n16

Lansbury, Coral, 6n15
Lawrence, George Alfred, 127
Leavis, Q. D., 50, 86, 146
Lee, Nelson, 4
Leech, John, 66
Lemon, Mark, 4, 159
Lewes, George Henry, 108
Lewis, M. G., 80n16
Littlewood, S. R., 144
Lover. *See* Dandy (or Wicked) Lover
Luke the Labourer (Buckstone), 39

MacDonald, Susan, 131n3
Maclise, Daniel, 54n14, 107
Magic Flute (Mozart), 52
Malevolent Spirit, 172
Malone Dies (Beckett), 165

188 Index

Malory, Thomas, 128n30
Manning, Sylvia, 85
Marcus, Stephen, 157
Marriage theme, 2, 77, 85, 107; and heroine's passivity, 130, 136; and hero's guilt, 111, 117; and parent-child relation, 80, 84–87; and social class, 99, 118; and unsuitable partners, 16–18, 30, 66, 69, 73, 82, 147–148
Mayer, David, 91, 127n27, 152–154
Medvedev, P. N., 21
Meisel, Martin, 20, 24, 41–42, 85, 173
Melodrama, 22, 25–29, 31; aesthetic value of, 32–33; characters in, 93, 102, 127, 143–144; conservatism of, 36–37; and Dandy Lover, 93, 96, 98, 101; French, 26, 28, 34; heroes in, 105, 120, 127, 143–144; heroines in, 143–144; and interchange of genres, 93, 102; and morality, 36–37, 155; and pantomime, 26–38; and plot, 1, 32–35, 37, 39, 83, 102; and realism, 39–40; relation with pantomime, 102, 143, 154–155; romantic, 28; social, 28, 34, 36; as vehicle of protest, 33–34, 36, 38–39, 93, 101; and vengeance, 31; villains in, 101–102, 104, 143–144, 174; worldview of, 34, 44
Melville, Herman, 40, 127
Memoirs of Joseph Grimaldi, 4–5, 14, 15, 69, 148, 169
Merry Wives of Windsor (Shakespeare), 159
Micromania (Dewey), 25
Miller, J. Hillis, xi, 5, 130, 136, 161n24
Milton, John, 101
Mise-en-scène. *See* Stage settings
Moby Dick (Melville), 127
Moers, Ellen, 95
Moncrieff, Scott, 89n25
Monod, Sylvère, 49, 106, 125
Morality, 16, 20; and carnival, 41; and character development, 51–55, 57, 60, 65–66, 84, 121, 137–139, 142, 145, 164, 166, 177; and Clown, 20, 41; and fantasy, 55;

and guilt, 111–113, 115, 117–118, 133–134; and melodrama, 36–37; in melodrama, 155; in pantomime, 155; and pious fraud, 52–55, 60, 137, 177; and plot, 31, 41, 45, 178; and revolution, 36; and self-interest, 84, 86; and sentimentality, 38; and skepticism, 62–63; and social aspiration, 99
Morley, Henry, 25
Morley, John, 1n2, 49n2
Morrison, Arthur, 37
Morton, John M., 23n5
Mozart, Wolfgang Amadeus, 52
Mundhenk, Rosemary, 58n21

Narrative. *See* Plot
Needham, Gwendolyn, 50
Nemesis, 148
New Comedy, 8, 11, 19, 69
Newman, John Henry, 97
Newsom, Robert, 171
Nietzsche, Friedrich, 100
Nigger of the Narcissus (Conrad), 33
No Name (Collins), 55n14
Novel of development, English, 50–51, 65. *See also Bildungsroman*
Nursery rhymes, 47, 49

Oddie, William, 159
Oedipus complex, 75, 135
Oliphant, Margaret, 6, 126, 128
Olshin, Toby, 19n45
Oppenlander, Ella Ann, 5n12
Orwell, George, 36, 45, 106–107, 129–130, 159n18
Othello (Shakespeare), 63–64

Pantaloon, x, 2–3, 5, 13, 15–16, 22, 24, 68, 121, 144, 148; amorous propensities of, 73; as authority figure, 154–155; Dandy Lover changed to, 91; Lady Dedlock as, 172; William Dorrit as, 173; Fagin as, 72; Thomas Gradgrind as, 172; Arthur Gride as, 73–74; Dr. Manette as, 173; Mrs. Markleham as, 79–83, Edward Murdstone as, 141; Ralph Nickleby as, 17, 156; Pecksniff as, 72, 83; Daniel Peggotty as, 86–90; Pickwick as, 7–8,

17, 72; relation with Clown, 70, 72, 74, 151–152, 154, 156; Scrooge as, 72; Mr. Spenlow as, 74, 76–79; as villain, 69–70, 72–74, 76, 86, 90; Mr. Wardle as, 7, 17; Mr. Wickfield as, 83–86

Pantomime: and acting, ix; characters in, 2, 11, 14–16, 26, 69, 93, 102, 127, 143–144; as children's theater, ix–x, 4, 178; Christmas, ix–1, 4, 10, 12, 15, 20, 141–142, 178; and comedy, xi, 2–3, 8–9, 11; and commedia dell'arte, 119; and Dickens' writings on, 5, 13–16, 69, 73n10, 109–110, 121, 160; Easter, 10; and everyday life, 13–15; financial support for, ix, 1n2; French, ix, 10, 144–145; and interchange of genres, 22, 25, 40–41, 45, 93, 102; modern, 47; and morality, 155; pious fraud in, 67; and plot, 1–3, 22–23, 45, 76, 83, 102, 130, 152, 161; and realism, 67; Regency, 2, 17, 47, 91, 120, 152, 172; relation with melodrama, 1, 25–27, 102, 143, 154–155; rhymed verse in, 23; Roman, ix; and sexuality, ix, 105; and social critique, 11–12; topical allusions in, 24–25; and transformation, 41–42, 44, 47, 60–61, 102, 178; and Victorian period, 2, 13; and violence, 15; writers of, 1n2, 3n6, 4

Paradise Lost (Milton), 101

Parent-child relation, 74–76, 79–80, 82–86, 98–99, 173

Patriarchy, 131, 156

Pepys, Samuel, 123

"Phiz" (pseud. H. K. Browne), 107–108

Pierrot, 144–145, 149, 156n12, 174

Pious Fraud, 53–68

Planché, James Robinson, 1–4, 7, 22–23, 91, 102–104

Plautus, Titus Maccius, 19

Plot, x; and absurdism, 3; and audience, 23; and catharsis, 32; and character development, 60, 65–66, 68, 137–139, 142, 145, 164, 166, 177; and characters, 2, 93, 102; and classical unity, 25; and comedy, 2, 64; and fantasy, 23; and fate of villains, 104; and female viewpoint, 141; and happy ending, 32, 44, 104, 161, 177; and harlequinade, 3; and interchange of genres, 26–30, 32, 38–40, 45–46, 61, 102; and melodrama, 1, 32–35, 37, 39, 83, 102; and morality, 31, 41, 45, 178; and motivation, 83; and pantomime, 2–3, 22, 23, 45, 76, 83, 102, 130, 152, 161; and pious fraud, 55, 57–58, 60–67, 108, 137, 142, 177; and reader response, 45, 58–60, 62, 65; and realism, 23, 39; and reconciliation, 104; and rhetoric, 32, 34; and sentimentality, 32, 35, 64; and sexuality, 143–144; and status of hero, 143–144; and status of heroine, 133; and status of villain, 144; and transformation scene, 60–61; and vengeance, 31, 35

Poe, Edgar Allan, 55n16

Polhemus, Robert, 72

Political protest: and carnival, 41; Dickens' ambivalence toward, 101; and melodrama, 34–36, 93; and *ressentiment*, 100–101

Poole, Elizabeth, 123

Povey, Eliza, 123n20

Pratt, Branwen, 16, 147n6, 175n6

Praz, Mario, 127

Prendergast, Christopher, 34, 36–37, 39, 102

Priestley, J. B., 157, 166

Principal Boy, 123, 126, 141, 160

Protestantism, 12

Psychology: of characters, 8, 135–136; and criticism, xi; and guilt, 113, 117; of harlequinade, 155

Punch and Judy show, 15

Punch (periodical), 159

Puritanism, 13

Rahill, Frank, 26n16

Reader response, 45, 58–60, 62, 65, 101–102, 105, 151–152, 162, 169, 171, 177; and identification with characters, 107–111, 116, 125, 128, 136–139, 141–142

Realism, 11, 16, 23–25, 36, 39–40,

Realism (continued)
  50–51, 55, 62, 67, 142, 171, 177;
  and pious fraud, 51–55, 57, 60
Religion, 10, 130, 136, 149–150
Restoration drama, 101
Rhetoric, 32, 34
Rich, John, 22
Richardson, Samuel, 101
Richardson the Showman, 4, 12–13
Richard III (Shakespeare), 33
Robinson Crusoe (Morley), 1n2
Robinson Crusoe (Sheridan), 22
Rodolph the Wolf (Planché), 91, 102, 104
Romance literature, 52–53
Roman *pantomimus*, ix
Romeo and Juliet (Shakespeare), 33
Rousseau, Jean-Jacques, 53–54

Sala, George Augustus, 4
Sartor Resartus (Carlyle), 51
Satire, 11, 21, 28, 91
Saturnalia, 10, 152
Schilling, Bernard, 159–161
Schlicke, Paul, 12, 18, 20, 145, 157
Scott, Walter, 138
Sentimentality, 32, 35–38, 44, 64, 136–137, 163–164, 166
Sexuality, ix; and Benevolent Agent, 47; and Clown, 171, 174; and Dandy Lover, 93, 118, 174; Dickens' views on, 84–85; and family, 45, 85; and Harlequin, 123, 125; and harlequinade, 44; of heroes, 128–129; of heroines, 133–135; and pantomime, 105, 123, 125; and parent-child relation, 84–87; and plot, 143–144
Shakespeare, William, 14, 19, 33, 57–58, 62–67, 126n24, 137, 139, 157, 159–160, 163–164
Shaw, George Bernard, 6–8, 105, 116–117, 130–131, 146–147
Shelley, Percy Bysshe, 166–167
Sheridan, Richard, 22
Shuckburgh, John, 157n17
Skepticism, 62–63, 83, 86
Slater, Michael, 49, 108n6
Sleeping Beauty, 126
Smith, Adam, 38

Smith, Grahame, 33–34, 58, 62, 77
Smith, Peter, 85n21
Society: class in, 93–100, 106, 118, 152, 155, 177; criticism of, 11–12, 34–36, 39, 41, 44, 60, 93–95, 101, 154, 162–163, 177–178; family in, 44–45; hierarchy in, 90, 93, 125, 163, 173; institutions of, 44; patriarchal, 131
Spectator (periodical), 55
Spencer, Herbert, 53–54
Spilka, Mark, 11
Stage settings, 3, 11, 23–24, 41–42, 44, 121, 178
Stanfield, Clarkson, 4
Stark, Myra, 131n3
Stephen, James Fitzjames, 106, 128, 142, 167
Stewart, Garrett, 96, 165
Stone, Harry, 52, 101n8
Storey, Robert F., 10n29, 156n12
Sucksmith, Harvey Peter, 163
Supernatural. *See* Fantasy

Tempest (Shakespeare), 164
Tennyson, Alfred, 97, 127–129
Terence, 19
Thackeray, William Makepeace, x, 59–60, 62, 109, 128, 162
Theater, x, 3–4, 11, 25, 41–42, 57, 67, 101, 119, 127; Dickens' novels adapted for, 72n5; financed by pantomime, ix; and genre, 32, 39
Tillotson, Kathleen, 169n2
Time Machine (Wells), 79
Tolstoy, Lev Nikolayevich, 33
Tom Jones (Fielding), 51, 138, 139
Tomlin, E. W. F., 163n29
Tragedy, 21, 33, 63, 157, 174
Trojan Women (Euripides), 33
Trollope, Anthony, 58–59, 65, 109

Vestris, Lucia Elizabeth, 123
Vicar of Wakefield (Goldsmith), 57
Villains, 26, 28, 39, 69, 72–74, 76, 83, 91, 94, 98–99, 112, 129; and genre, 102; in melodrama, 174; narrative status of, 144; relation with Clown, 150, 152; relation with heroines, 143; as rescuers,

148, 151; and *ressentiment*, 100–101, 105; and sexuality, 105; as victims, 101–102
Violence, 10, 15, 37, 125–126, 155, 178

Walpole, Horace, 22
War and Peace (Tolstoy), 33
Waverley (Scott), 138
Webster, John, 33
Weinstein, Philip M., 87
Wells, H. G., 79
Welsh, Alexander, 130, 136
Westburg, Barry, 96
Whitaker, Muriel, 128n30
Whittington, Dick, 94
Wicked Lover. *See* Dandy (or Wicked) Lover
Wilde, Oscar, 38
Wilhelm Meister (Goethe), 51, 65–66
Williams, Merryn, 75, 141n11

Wilson, A. E., 10, 154
Winter's Tale (Shakespeare), 57, 62–63
Wiston, J., 143
Woffington, Peg, 123
Wolfe, Charles, 6n15
Worldview, 133, 142, 174; of comedy, 32; and genre, 21–22, 25–26, 32, 38–40; of harlequinade, 44; of melodrama, 26, 32, 34, 39, 44; and narrative coherence, 39–40; of pantomime, 26; and realism, 39; transformation of, 60–61, 64, 68, 84
Worth, George J., 28–29, 33
Wuthering Heights (Brontë), 127

Yeats, William Butler, 151, 167n36
Yellow Dwarf, 19

Zanbrano, A. L., 6n15
Zola, Émile, 24

OHIO UNIVERSITY LIBRARY

Please return this book as soon as you have finished with it. In order to avoid a fine it must be returned by the latest date stamped below.

NON-UNIV
FEB 23 1990

RETURN BY
DEC 05 1998

FEB 25 1990 NOV 23 1998

NON. UNIV.
MAR 11 1990

MAR 12 1990

MAR 26 1993